"The book [Clear the Space...F [barcode] has power and life in the w~~~~~ ~~~~, ~ ~~~~~~ ~~~~ ~~, ~~ ~ a tremendous book! Everybody should have at least one..."

~ **Larry Quell, DC**

"I love Connie's 'whole person' approach to decluttering. It is impossible for us to do better than our thinking will allow. So often people attempt to declutter by using will power and muscling through it. This approach seldom works and even when it does, it is usually not sustainable, because the physical clutter is a side effect of the mental and emotional clutter. Connie's book helps people to address clutter on all levels, which greatly increases the odds for success and positive change."

~ **Jonathan Manske, author of**
The Law of Attraction Made Simple

"Exhilaration is waiting for us, and *Clear the Space...Feel the Rush* is the concise road map to get us there sooner rather than later! The author wisely segmented this delightful book between decluttering the mind, body, and stuff so the reader can immediately address what is individually most pressing. Reading this insightful and informative book blossomed into the real life changes I have longed to realize!"

~ **Ronda Steinke-McDonald, Author of**
What the Soul Wants for Christmas, Open Yourself to Fresh
Celebrations of the Holidays...and Life

"Joyfully written, easy to read, the light-hearted encouragement and the abundance of techniques makes "Feeling the Rush" an attainable goal for anyone. The footnotes and references allow the reader to delve deeper into specific techniques for decluttering the mind and body."

~ Robbie Zephirin, Retired Civil Engineer

"I realized 'The Rush,' is the big deal in all this, and that making the effort to go ahead and achieve things I've been procrastinating on gives, not only the immediate feeling of satisfaction, but also improves my health through the rush (endorphins)!"

~ Kelly Reifsnider, Pilates Instructor

"This book is super relatable and fun to read. The author is a unique character and her approach to decluttering is thorough and refreshing! I highly recommend this book to both organizing/decluttering fanatics, as well as newbies who just need that one nugget or impetus to get started and keep going!"

~ Angela Schnaubelt, Marketing Strategist for Alternative Health Care Practitioners

"Connie has been the most productive person I know! She always has an answer for any question regarding the processes of organizing, planning, and effective solutions for personal health. I'm glad that she has decided to share with us all. This book is the culmination of Connie's wisdom in dealing with this often confusing and scattered world and our place in it!"

~ Robin Korn, Professional Organizer, Certified Senior Advisor, Space Wranglers, LLC

Dear Reader,

In *Clear the Space… Feel the Rush*, Connie Ellefson shares over 15 years of experience in working with others to declutter and downsize their lives. Connie's passion for simplicity is infectious. When you feel 'the rush' that Connie shares, you'll be motivated to find more ways to live a simpler, lighter, and more gentle existence. If your life feels like a constant effort (as mine often did), it's time to lighten your load.

The reasons we struggle to downsize and declutter go far beyond the 'stuff' we acquire over time. Beyond the physical realm, Connie reveals how the clutter we accumulate over time can become toxic to our body, mind, and spirit.

Much of 'the work' we need to do runs counter to the pervasive marketing aimed at consuming more (and more). Connie reveals why 'less is more' and shows us the path to greater peace and happiness through less. The call to action is to 'upcycle' all areas of your life, reevaluate your choices, find greater appreciation for all you have, and rediscover the joy and enthusiasm within.

Note: Akin to coffee and conversation with a trusted friend (rather than an authority pontificating advice), her playful choice of words makes the reading experience more enjoyable (albeit slightly different from what you may be used to).

With sincere gratitude,

PS: We would be grateful for *your* feedback or suggestions on how to improve or enhance this work. We invite you to share your feedback anonymously via the QR code to the left or at:
www.ClearTheSpace.com/feedback

Praise for Clear the Space

"I really liked the humorous aspects. I've been a travel nurse for 3 months and the book made me think about all the stuff I have at home that I really didn't need. It should help a lot of people realize they're not alone in this cluttered world. You will feel like there's more space around you to breathe in the air!"

~ Roxanne Rodriguez, RN

"I enjoyed this book and got a lot out of it for myself. As I read it, I could see a means to be set free from the many facets and entanglements of stuff, both literal and figurative. The mind is a cluttered mess we spend a lifetime defending, excusing and frankly ignoring. It's a lot easier coasting along rather than trying to fix the darn thing, so we keep coasting our lives away."

**~ Joyce Leake, Animal Communicator
and Horse Trainer**

"I highly recommend it. It will give you a new freedom in your life. Plus it is an easy read and very fun to read. Good information and a reminder to clear the clutter in and around your life. Buy it you will enjoy your life more!"

~ Blase deRoco, Mortgage Broker

"Never would I have thought that reading a book about decluttering could be fun. However, Connie Ellefson magically makes it so. No judgements, no hard fast rules. Just honest, self-pacing advice that puts a smile on my face every time I turn a page."

~ Nancy Griffin, Realtor

CLEAR THE SPACE...
FEEL THE RUSH

Declutter Body, Mind, and Stuff
To Reclaim Energy, Freedom, and Fun

By
Connie Lockhart Ellefson

ClearTheSpace.com

v9.16

Cover design by Tatiana Villa
Produced by Brian Schwartz for Wise Media Group

ATTENTION CORPORATIONS, UNIVERSITIES, COLLEGES, AND PROFESSIONAL ORGANIZATIONS

Quantity discounts are available on bulk purchases of this book for educational or gift purposes. Special books or book excerpts can also be created to fit specific needs.

Please visit **www.ClearTheSpace.com** for inquiries.

DEDICATION

In alphabetical order...Ben, Ian, Jamie, Jenn, Joey, River—my great loves!

And to Nik Scott, professional blogging expert who said, when I told her what my book was about, "OK, so I need you to get this done right now!"

CONTENTS

How refreshing is the whinny of the pack horse,
relieved of all burden.

-Zen saying

INTRODUCTION

Feeling the Rush

Have you ever had that scrumptious, tingling feeling from reorganizing and sorting out an area of your possessions? Especially when it included getting rid of some of that stuff?

If you've done any decluttering, versus simply reorganizing, you know what I'm talking about. It could be a room, a closet, or even your glove compartment.

Did you notice what happened when you started weeding out the fuzzy edges of your riffraff belongings, seeing the back of the closet, not just what's jammed in at the front, found a glimmer of the edge sharpening between the loved items and the unloved detritus?

There's an exhilarating rush—a feeling of freedom and accomplishment.

And didn't you feel at least a little bit…high?

Not going to lie, one reason I took up professional organizing fifteen years ago was due to that high!

For me it happens. Every. Single. Time.

And it doesn't even have to be my own stuff. I feel the rush of energy from clearing out any old space, even if it belongs to one of my clients.

But we know that. We've watched the shows, read the books, or simply seen a super-organized parent or friend in action with the secrets we'd love to learn. We may have even felt a vicarious thrill from seeing other peoples' spaces transformed.

That's the rush! That's the fun side of decluttering and organizing your stuff. Unfortunately, it usually comes at the end of the process, long after we've climbed over the big boulder of reluctance blocking our efforts to let go of our belongings. How can it be fun all the way through? How can we shrink that boulder down to a pebble? And how do we overcome the challenge of simply getting started?

Scientific studies show that decluttering and organizing can relieve stress, help you focus, feel calmer, and get out of a rut.[1,2,3]

I have to confess—I am a recovering "organizing book" junkie. Each time I gave in to the allure of a shiny new organizing book, I dreamed of a life of order and ease, convinced "this one at last" would magically transform my life! With each new method, I'd tuck into decluttering and organizing with great enthusiasm and inspiration. I experienced the exhilaration of the pack horse mentioned above.

I'd make a lot of progress—*almost* completing the task, but eventually dwindling down and stopping. Or I'd finally get everything sorted out, but it wouldn't stay that way for long. Often, I'd be too depressed or tired to care.

What was missing?

It's Not Just About the "Stuff" Clutter

Fortunately, though I tried to quit the organizing books cold turkey, a few still slipped past my guard, and these started to hint

---

[1] Saxbe DE, Repetti R. No place like home: home tours correlate with daily patterns of mood and cortisol. Pers Soc Psychol Bull. 2010 Jan;36(1):71-81. doi:10.1177/0146167209352864. PMID: 19934011.

[2] Indiana University. Tidier homes, fitter bodies. https://newsinfo.iu.edu/web/page/normal/14627.html

[3] https://www.mayoclinic.org/healthy-lifestyle/stress-management/in-depth/how-decluttering-your-space-could-make-you-healthier-and-happier/art-20390064

at what I was suspecting. It isn't only about the stuff (possessional clutter)!

What if there's more to it than simply applying better storage and downsizing methods? There must be a deeper secret to getting organized.

The "stuff" is what's most visible, and it looks like the obvious culprit, so that's what we focus on and spend an ocean of time and energy trying to get all sorted out. We hope, hope, hope it will change everything and stay that way for good.

But why did I always stop the process at the 90% mark? Why did I drag my feet so long to get started in the first place? Why was it so very difficult to let go of items any kind friend would simply dropkick into the dumpster?

It was then the lightbulb lit. The possessional clutter is only the tip of the iceberg! Below the waterline, the mind clutter (thoughts and emotions) that creates it is far, far vaster than the "stuff" clutter.

If we're honest, we also have to accept that sometimes we don't freaking feel like sorting, deciding, discarding, decluttering, and organizing because we're simply too tired, undernourished, or under-exercised. Surprising, I know, to think we could be undernourished with the cornucopia of food available to most of us lucky enough to live where we can afford items we don't need. But a steady diet of additive-filled foods can leave us deficient in key energy-giving nutrients. This is physical body clutter slowing down our efforts to declutter mind and stuff and hampering our ability to enjoy our lives.

An Alternate Approach to Decluttering

What if there was a way to unclutter your life that went beyond simply reorganizing your random belongings, yet again? What if we could *start somewhere else* in our efforts to get decluttered and organized?

After all, if you shake off the doldrums with a little energizing exercise, it's easier to dig into the junk drawers that need sorting. Let go of a long-standing emotional/mental block and see what else you could let go of. Round up a few items to donate and the thrill of release lightens your mood.

Thus, the idea for this book was born, with the aim of being different than any other organizing book: a collection of ideas for coming in any of those three doors (body, mind, or stuff) to declutter that which doesn't serve us, then move on to other refreshing changes in our lives!

The cool part is we don't have to sort out *all* those clutter realms in order to be decluttered and organized. Since they're interwoven, you can start anywhere you like among the three, and changes will start automatically happening in the other two!

The next question is, "How to make it fun?" After all, most of us don't relish the thought of wading into all those unmade decisions (stuff clutter), suiting up to work out and get tired (body clutter), or wrestling with our mental and emotional roadblocks (mind clutter.) That's what makes it so hard to get started at all.

I realized there's one perk that kicks in right away in any of those realms—it's the rush!

And it doesn't just happen when you declutter your stuff! It also happens when you release those tiresome emotions that drag you down! It happens when you declutter your body—which then feels frisky and exhilarated to be free of toxins and other dead weight!

So that makes it fun in the moment, but what about the long term?

4

Decluttering to Create Your Dream Life

Take a page out of the professional organizer's manual and ignore the stuff stacked around everywhere for a while. Whether you're living your dream life, spending your time as you want to, and living in your home or office as you would like to, ask yourself, "What's my vision for my life?"

By focusing on the life you'd like to create, it becomes crystal clear which of your possessions are supporting your dream life and which are sabotaging it.

When I asked my 80-something stepfather how he'd like to spend more of his time, he instantly had the answer: "I'd like to build more model ships."

He realized that having most of the flat surfaces in his house covered with piles of paperwork he felt duty bound to deal with wasn't conducive to that dream. He began systematically taking steps to get control of the paper and cut it off at the source.

This is a possessional dream, of which there are thousands, billions, even when you consider the unique viewpoint of each person in the world!

A dream that inspires physical body decluttering might include things such as eliminating a health challenge, being able to dance the tango, or waking up feeling frisky more days than not.

The dream of an emotionally uncluttered life will also often be an ongoing one. A dream to feel more peaceful or courageous is lifelong, and to some extent always a challenge, due to the nature of being human.

Having that shining light in front of you inspires you in an exciting way, and a thousand times more effectively than beating yourself up for not being there already.

Short term fun? Check.

Long term reward? Check.

Who knew how much power there was in simply taking out the trash, so to speak??

You're going to hear "Make it fun, and it's more likely to get done," quite a lot. I consider life one big science project with infinite experiments available for your enjoyment. Look on this whole "clear the space" process as just one of the many ways to experiment with life, then you'll supercharge its enjoyment that much more!

Decluttering versus Organizing

Which do you find easier, decluttering (downsizing, getting rid of, minimizing) or organizing (arranging the pared-down items in a beneficial, orderly way)?

For most of us, hands down, it's the decluttering that gets the best of us. It's simply so, so hard to let go of our stuff, no matter how useless, unlovely, and unloved some of it may be.

Sooooo, just so you know, this book is much more about decluttering than organizing. My thought was, "Why clutter up a lot of pages with what has already been said so magnificently in dozens of other books about organizing?" Especially since it's really the decluttering that's the harder of the two, isn't it? Deciding what to delete brings up a lot of resistance, while figuring out how to organize what's left—not exactly rocket science, eh?

Is it rude to say, "A child of three could do it"?

The truth is, a child of three *can* sort items and put them away where they belong. Letting go of that set of blocks, though? Not so easy.

However, my favorite organizing tips, pared down by the test of time, are still included here, plus a few you may not have heard of before.

There are multiple options to take that first step into either decluttering your thoughts/emotions (mind), your physical being (body), or your possessions (stuff).

Some tips are very intuitive, as in "Yes, I've heard this before. Tell me something I didn't know." Perhaps these examples will strike a chord you have not heard before and help move you over the threshold with that first step. Other suggestions are less well-known and will give you new experiments to try in the game of life and letting go.

(Including "what's good about clutter"...What??)

This book is divided into four main sections and a summary section (with a secret bonus tip at the end!):

Part I – Declutter Basics: Introductory material that applies to all kinds of decluttering, how you'll experience "the rush" no matter which door you choose to enter first, and just how beneficial the rush is. Turns out there's a lot more to it than just feeling buzzed!

The next three sections help you recognize the clutter and decide which you want to tackle first.

Part II – Clear the Mind Clutter: Mental & Emotional

Part III – Clear the Possessional Clutter: Your Belongings, Your 'Stuff'

Part IV – Clear the Body Clutter

Part V – The Big View: Final Thoughts

There are many topics and ideas offered, and many are like brief introductions. Whatever appeals to you can be researched in greater depth with the help of the resources section at the end, or through your own online searches.

Declutter on Your Own Terms

You can read through the whole book and go back to the area that appeals most to you. Or, because each section stands on its own, you can save time by simply reading the beginning section and the area that interests you most, be it body, mind, or stuff.

By the end of the book, you should have several strategies that inspire the unique person you are to get started with decluttering, organizing your life, and jumpstarting your dreams!

If nothing else, it's my hope you'll come away with at least these four messages:

1. Decluttering and organizing are worth the time it takes, several times over, in the rush of energy, enjoyment, and lightness they bring out in you!
2. "First, declutter the guilts." Guilt is the best first thing to toss on this decluttering journey. Feeling guilty is almost always about the past, over which you have zero power to change. Don't waste a second beating yourself up about how you've gotten to where you have with your clutter, whatever it may be. Focus on what you can change, and what tickles your fancy to get started with. Plus, how can you have the fun of creating the "after" if you don't have a "before" to compare it to??
3. Decluttering and organizing are part of an ongoing journey, part of the flow of life, not a one-stop event. You see this most clearly in physical decluttering; it's not hard to realize you don't exercise or eat right once and you're good to go! Similarly, stresses and challenges are never going to stop coming at you and your thoughts and emotions; it's about learning to manage how you respond to them. And new things are likely to keep

showing up in your home—unless you completely give up shopping and gift-receiving. As if!! (See point no. 2)

4. Last, but not least: Make it fun, and it's more likely to get done! A good dose of humor, and not taking yourself or the situation too seriously, will go a long way in not only speeding up the decluttering process, but also immeasurably adding to the richness of your time on earth!

My aim is to encourage rather than lay down the law. Let's face it: it's an ingrained human tendency to take on more than we can easily handle. ("You crazy kids!") It's a chief ingredient in hope and in the desire to grow, those basic, yet powerful human drives.

It's also an ingrained human tendency to resist doing what people tell you you "should/must" do, even if it's yourself doing the telling, which is reason #2 I don't lay down the law. Try testing it right now. Tell yourself you have to do something. See how you react. Crazy, right? That's why I only cheerlead (with a few possible exceptions…).

Before you do anything else with this book, write down at least one dream (or many) that you've given up on and that you would like to work toward again. Keep it in mind as you read through the decluttering tips and make notes of suggestions to apply.

It's said we can never stop a bad habit (and certainly not in one step, like a New Year's resolution), but only replace it with a better one. So, while you're at it, list new habits you'd like to adopt to support your specific dreams.

And remember, the dream is a powerful motivator that will crystallize your focus and draw you forward!

PART I
DECLUTTER BASICS

Raised by a Decluttering Supermom

Since I just said, "First, let's declutter the guilts," I offer this story to let you know no one is immune to changing their stuff-gathering ways. With my dad working for an oil company, I grew up moving about every six months to a year, either to a different town, or a different house, as often happened, when a landlord sold our house out from under us.

My first six years were spent living in a trailer. Truth was we could simply tape up the drawers and head out when we moved without having to do anything else. But what stuck with me, besides the pain of saying goodbye to my little friends each and every time, was that even when we still lived in the trailer, Mom made us systematically junk out our possessions to lighten the load with every move.

Our first trailer, which fit our family of four, was eight feet wide by forty-three feet long (344 sq. ft) and it never seemed that crowded, so you know our belongings were few! Eventually the homes got bigger, but the habit of "junking out" continued.

All through college, I still traveled light. Any new item in my life was scrutinized with an eye towards whether I could easily pack it into the sturdy old dynamite boxes (about the size of a document storage box) which were relics of my childhood.

I also needed to be able to carry it myself. I never had the courage to ask people for moving help--also a leftover from my younger days. I had an entrenched horror of having too many things, always thinking ahead to my next move.

The habit stuck with me. When I finished college and moved to Denver to seek my fortune, I carried everything I owned, including a ten-speed bicycle and two large speakers stashed, with room to spare, in my old Chevy Impala.

"Travel light," was my motto, ever and always!

Fast forward six years: My husband-at-the-time and I moved house with our two little kids. It took me and five big guys four and a half hours to load all our stuff into a big moving van! With shock and disbelief, I cried out to God and everybody, "What happened??!!"

I started working on figuring it out and downsizing from that day on. I had seen with my own eyes how easy it is to go off the "travel light" track!

The Seeds of *Clear the Space*

In 2008, after my civil engineering occupation and the faltering economy had brought me four layoffs in six years, I said to myself, "Call me crazy, but thinking might be time for a new career."

Remembering I'd gotten much more satisfaction out of organizing and clearing up my desk at the office than doing the work itself, I decided to give professional organizing a go. A name for my biz didn't come easily; for a couple of months, I discarded many versions of "Streamlining your Life," and vague references to "sailing into your future." (Living in land-locked Colorado I've only ever sailed a leaf down a stream.)

On a Tuesday afternoon about 4:30 pm, as I stared out the window from my dining table, the words "Clear the Space" showed up, unbidden, in my head. I knew it was a message straight from the heavens, and that it meant something a lot bigger than organizing my sock drawer! I gave my new company that name, and I have been intrigued, inspired, and amused by the words ever since.

It seemed an open-ended phrase that could have endless connotations. It wasn't the same as "clear space," or "clear a space." It hinted at meanings I didn't yet know, beyond what I knew of organizing then—purging your belongings of the dumb stuff, and storing the remaining "beautiful, useful and beloved" items in a way that makes your life easier.

You can pick your own meaning: clear the space for your creative, productive life; for your dreams to materialize; for you to know yourself and loved ones better; for your friends to find a welcoming haven at your house; for your joy to expand; or for your skateboard to have its own parking space in the house! Whatever. Mainly, clear the space for you to be you, which is the best contribution you can make to this life!

"Feel the Rush!" – What it's about

It turns out the good feeling of the rush doesn't just appear out of thin air. It has an actual physical effect on your body. Have you heard of endorphins, the feel-good chemicals that circulate through your body and help relieve pain or stress? You might have noticed them when you eat food that's just the right amount of spicy for you, enough to wake up your taste buds, but not enough to get into the painful range.

A few minutes later you feel like pounding your fist on the table and saying "Yeah, that's some good chili!" Your brain has registered the heat on your tongue, and whether it hurts you or not, it sends out endorphins to relieve the pain. That's why you feel good! And that's a small taste of the rush.

You may have heard of endorphins in relation to exercise. They're famous for starting to course through your system after you exercise for about 30 minutes in a row. This is partly why some get addicted to exercise, believe it or not.

Technically speaking, endorphins are neurotransmitters. They transmit messages along your nerves using electrical impulses, but the bottom line is: endorphins make you feel delicious, like you're in the middle of getting a massage! Another neurotransmitter, serotonin, helps you feel "happy," and is famous, too, for being in short supply when you feel depressed. You also may have heard of dopamine, the more hard-edged pleasurable-feeling chemical related to desire, that can come from indulging in alcohol, drugs, and video games (not kidding, that's why they're addictive--TV watching is in there, too, sorry to say).

Whether it's endorphins, serotonin, or some other neurotransmitter[4] that rises up in your body after a good bout of decluttering, these chemicals are what cause the exhilaration ("the rush") you feel from it.

Related to the rush is the Chinese practice of feng shui, the art of placing objects in your environment to harmonize with your own energy. Feng shui practice is about much more than decluttering, but one of its main ideas is that stagnant energy is released when clutter is cleared out. Feng shui speaks more about the interplay between you and the objects, but still, you're part of the circuit.

So, I'm thinking we could call it part of the rush as well, especially because decluttering is almost always a first step in applying feng shui principles.

As an example of how we interact with our stuff, our eyes can't help but be caught by every item out of place as we walk

---

[4] Timesaver: I don't want to keep writing "endorphins, serotonin, or dopamine" over and over, any more than you want to keep reading it. So, for simplicity's sake, I'm just going to call them endorphins, OK?

through a room, or even just glance around. This scrambles our focus and distracts us; our brain stops momentarily to think about where that item really should be and wonders whether or not to put it away right now. Or now. Oh, how 'bout right now?

Each day our decision-making ability can only handle so much before it needs to rest and refresh; wasting it stewing on the clutter cuts down on what's available for something more creative. Cortisol, the stress hormone, also circulates in your body when you are irritated by the stuff out of place, further diminishing your current creativity or problem-solving potential by taking you into fight-or-flight mode.

By contrast, the rush of an uncluttered space is a gift that keeps on giving. For days after, you can revisit the cleared space and feel the refreshing energy all over again. Delicious rush!

Scratching your head about this? Thinking, "I've never felt that rush in my life… Or at least not about clearing out a closet!" For you it might show up in a different way, a little more enthusiasm for finishing a task, a little more enjoyment, a little more spring in your step. These are also signs of that energy released, and the life lightened.

Declutter Body, Mind and Stuff

As I mentioned, this book is laid out as I see clutter, in three interwoven aspects: possessional clutter (your things), physical body clutter, and mental/emotional clutter. Here's a quick rundown on what each means:

Mind Clutter – Mental/Emotional

Science estimates we think between 12,000 and 70,000 thoughts per day. At the very least, it's several per minute. Forget how fast we talk—the brain on its slowest day thinks way faster than the most seasoned motor-mouth.

15

Most of those thoughts (up to 95%[5]) are the same thoughts we thought yesterday, the day before, and the day before that. Unless we make a practice of trying out new ideas and habits, our thoughts may also be the same as they were a decade ago, which is why life sometimes seems like it doesn't change much. Many of those thoughts are negative, fearful, or at the very least, simply uselessly random.

Do *not* fear that I'm not going to tell you that you need to *stop that right now* and start thinking positively, or else! That way lies madness, and a lot of energy wasted attempting to stem the tide. Or worse, beating yourself up for not being able to do it.

The fact is, we can't control our thoughts. They simply keep barreling along at different rates of speed, but still nonstop. The more we try to stop them, the more overwhelmed we feel.

Though most of our thoughts are negative, it isn't the first time we think a negative thought that it starts doing its damage to our mood and courage. It's the 50th or 500th time in a row. The only thing we can do is drop negative thoughts without judging them before we get hooked into them and panic.

We can gently steer them towards something more productive. When you really get good at this, you'll be able to drop them with good humor in an instant: "Easy come, easy go."

A few examples of mind clutter include:

- Long-accepted limiting beliefs.
- Unwarranted fears (rarely justified - a 2005 Cornell University study[6] found 85% of what we worry about never happens, and among the feared events that do

---

[5] Tseng, J., Poppenk, J. Brain meta-state transitions demarcate thoughts across task contexts exposing the mental noise of trait neuroticism. *Nat Commun* 11, 3480 (2020). https://doi.org/10.1038/s41467-020-17255-9
[6] See *The Worry Cure* by Robert L. Leahy (2005) for more on this research.

happen, people often find there was a good lesson to be learned, or other benefit associated).

- Poor opinions of our bodies.
- Waking up in a bad mood from a crazy dream not even remembered.
- All the above, and dozens of other forms of mental/emotional clutter negatively impacting our emotions; most of it is our subconscious mind feeding our conscious thoughts.

It's big, man, and very cluttered! Clearing out a bit of the mental/emotional attic yields excellent dividends. The habits of favorite emotions (both "good" and "bad"), and knee-jerk reactions to almost everything that comes our way in life take up a ton of energy and time each day and are what lead to a lot of the same-old, same-old.

Bottom line: if the decluttering and organizing of your possessions never quite seems to get done, it's likely mind clutter holding you back.

There's good news about that, though. You may or may not have experienced an energy healing of your emotional blocks, but you've certainly enjoyed the stress relief that comes after a good cry, or finally telling a story you've kept bottled up to an empathic listener. These are energy releases, too. Coming from the "biggest part of the iceberg," emotional releases can be the biggest rush of all!

Possessional Clutter - Our Belongings, Our Stuff

Possessional clutter is generally obvious; that's why it's usually the prime target of most organizing strategies. All we need do is look around our spaces to experience the draining effects.

- Items piled up (those not part of the decorating scheme). Whether neatly or haphazardly, they likely indicate no plan has been made to store them effectively out of sight.
- Over-stuffed closets, drawers, or cabinets.
- (Possibly) the need to rent outside storage space when you're already living in your permanent home.
- Excessive time required to keep everything put away and organized.
- A feeling of dread when you think about entering your home or office.

Physical Body Clutter

Yikes! This is a subject that could get super-technical, with conditions such as arterial plaque, sluggish lymph systems, and inflammatory response potentially on the agenda.

Given that my training is in civil engineering and not medicine of any kind, we're sticking to the simple strategies in removing physical body clutter (whether toxins or just dead skin cells.)

Physical clutter may be evident in:

- Low energy.
- Headaches.
- Some unneeded weight (fat) you might be willing to release (Note: tongue-in-cheek).
- Allergies, skin problems, etc.
- Illnesses caused by toxins absorbed by skin and lungs, or from our food.

Physical decluttering, with its own kind of rush, will nevertheless provide exhilarating benefits in the short run (less lethargy, more energy, improved mood, etc.). In the long run, it may also benefit us by helping prevent many degenerative diseases we've come to consider a normal part of aging.

So, the rush is the fun part of decluttering, short-term deliciousness (endorphins) to go along with long-term payoffs. But however delightful this may be, it pales in comparison to the even bigger payoff.

The Real You Shines Through

At a business meet-up I heard two women discussing their desire to write a series of short books on their favorite subject, essential oils. One said, "We just need to get organized to write those books and get them published."

Like a thunderbolt, it hit me.

The whole point of getting decluttered and organized is not just to *be* organized, it's to *do* things!

We each have at least a handful of activities and dreams that speak to us and light us up from the inside. They could be sweetly simple or wildly ambitious and improbable.

We might dream of running a classroom, leading a boardroom, building airplane engines, repairing torn clothing, sweeping up the room or sweeping into a ballroom, keeping the account books or writing best-selling books, parasailing over a 1500-foot-deep canyon or tucking your kidlet into bed at night. (I know it sounds crazy, but my daughter-in-law did those last two in one day. The next day she returned to her beloved job as a dental hygienist, as per usual.)

It could even be sitting on the porch in the evening, quietly contemplating your garden with all your senses.

It's simply whatever unique combination of dreams, relentless desires, skills and topics that never fail to catch your attention and draw you in, with a hunger to go do that, be that, study that, handle that, achieve that, enjoy that.

Your desires, from the smallest ("Let's get everybody to breakfast on time") to the grandest (So, yeah, I desire to make art that changes the world for the better/travel to all the continents/nurture some gorgeous relationships") are all part of your hardwiring. They are the reason you are here: to be your astonishing self and move the world forward in your own unique way!

Clutter takes many forms: belongings, worries, ailments, over-packed schedules, lackluster entertainment, self-criticism, or favorite addictions. And whether the clutter's emotional, possessional, or in our physical bodies, it takes up energetic space in our lives. **Translation: Sometimes we use our clutter distractions as a convenient excuse to procrastinate on our dreams.**

Main Points and Purpose of the Book

- The whole point of getting decluttered and organized is not just to *be* organized, it's to *do* things!
- The real reason to clear the space in your life and in your soul is for the real you to shine through—to make the most of this life you've been given.
- You get to choose which form of clutter you clear first.
- No matter how you choose to start, before long, those endorphins will be swirling around inside you, making decluttering feel a lot more fun than it first sounded, eh? Long-term benefits and short-term deliciousness at your service!

At the very least, you can expect to:

1. Add 5–6 hours a week of free, unfettered time to your life.

2. Simplify routines, making your work, both at home and in your profession, more enjoyable.
3. Be in much better shape to deal with life's stresses.
4. Spend more of your time living in the present, the only place you have any real power.
5. Make room for the real you—your creativity, your best problem-solving skills, your unique contribution, and your fun.

Back to *The Rush*

It took a crazy long time to write this book, but it turns out it was just the right time (as it so often does.) Asked to give a last-minute talk, I quickly gave up my chicken-hearted excuses, realizing it gave me a perfect chance to crystallize my *Clear the Space* message.

Thanks to the time pressure and some recent info I had the biggest "Aha!" moment of this whole extended book-writing process.

I thought "clear the space" and "the real you shines through" was my main message, but I realized "the rush" was every bit as important, maybe even more so, with the benefits it provides.

I had recently read a very in-depth book, *Becoming Supernatural, How Common People are Doing the Uncommon*, by Dr. Joe Dispenza (chiropractor, neuroscience researcher, speaker, and contributor to movie *What the Bleep Do We Know.*) One key story gripped me. At a 4-day seminar he led in 2016, he asked 117 volunteers to take eight or nine minutes three times a day during each of the four days putting themselves in a high-vibrational frequency (a.k.a. positive) emotional state, such as happiness, gratitude, love, inspiration.

So, a little under thirty minutes a day of feeling happy.

At the beginning and end of the seminar, he tested them for Immunoglobulin A (IgA) levels in their systems. IgA is a protein present in the body which is one of the main indicators of the current strength of the person's immune system. At the end of the four days, the volunteers' IgA levels had risen an average of approximately 50%! As Dr. Dispenza stated, an increase in IgA such as this is significantly more effective in warding off disease than any flu shot or immune booster (supplement such as Vitamin C) people normally take to improve their immune system.

What else happens when we're happy, besides our immune system getting stronger? We experience "the rush" (which just plain feels good), stress hormones go down, we think more clearly, life's petty irritations bother us less, we see the good in people, we see the good in ourselves, and we come up with infinitely more creative solutions.

It isn't just about clearing the space that matters and isn't even just about the real you shining through.

The rush is equally important! The rush happens in each of the declutter areas. The endorphins are what make you feel happy and at peace. The rush isn't only about decluttering body, mind, and stuff; it's about the exponential release that happens when you declutter any aspect of your life, and how it opens up energy and time for your dreams and desires.

Talk about bang for your buck—the rush rules!

Here's to you and your fun game of clearing the space! As I said, you can start anywhere from here, Part II, III, or IV, but to me, mental and emotional clutter is the tail that wags the dog, so that's where I'm starting…

PART II
CLEAR THE MIND CLUTTER –
MENTAL & EMOTIONAL

You could reasonably ask, "Why go to all this trouble to declutter emotions? Don't I have enough to do yet? And anyway, isn't that just life?" One of my friends often says, "What's all this obsession with happiness crap? What's so bad about just allowing yourself to wallow in your negative emotions once in a while?"

She's right in one way, as resisting anything, including negative emotions, tends to make it stay around longer. That's a lot of what counseling and other healing techniques are about: letting yourself feel your emotions by giving yourself permission to talk about them, and thus, (hopefully) processing them and defusing their grip on your life. However, the payoff for everyday wallowing is small.

Researchers who study emotions and their effects on our lives say we can become addicted to our favorite negative emotions just as easily as we can to vodka or the shopping channels. Not only do they tend to keep us in a rut, but they also keep us rooted in the lizard brain, the amygdala (home of the fight-or-flight response mechanism, a.k.a. fear). This shuts off the reasoning and thinking parts of our brain, which could potentially come up with a solution to the problem or a different choice (not to mention simply enjoying our lives and having fun!).

According to Shawn Achor, author of *Before Happiness* and *The Happiness Advantage*, chronic unhappiness can cost us in our pocketbooks as well. He found that the companies where employees report higher levels of happiness at work have measurably higher profits, sometimes several times the profit margin of the companies with unhappy workers.[4]

You've probably come up with some doozy money-saving or money-making ideas on the home front as well as at work when you were in a happy, relaxed state. (And sure, you can also do that when totally under-the-gun crunched and stressed out, but the number of ideas, and the feeling that they could be accomplished, is ridiculously lower.)

How Do We Clear Mental and Emotional Clutter?

So, how in the world do we go about decluttering our emotions?

Anyone who has ever been tossed around on the sea of some wild, emotional upheaval feels like there's no way of controlling that, much less decluttering it. Even the lower-toned everyday emotions, like the tides, feel so inevitable and drearily ever-returning.

The experts tell us emotions are really all a wash of chemicals that arise in our bodies in reaction to hundreds of different stimuli. Actually, it's not really hundreds of stimuli, but only one.

Our thoughts.

Don't know about you, but that seems crazy to me. How can you not feel terrified seeing a meteor heading for your face, or relieved to the bottom of your soul at having turned in your last-ever college paper, or ecstatic at the sight of your favorite dessert sitting right there in front of you with room in your tummy to eat it?!

So, hmm, what, a thought like, "I am very likely to be in danger with this huge rock-like item approaching my exact coordinates at 400 feet per second"? Or "I like this baked product with a sugar-infused pumpkin mixture in the center, and intensely aerated dairy cream substance on top"?

I had to ponder this for a while to realize what I was missing was the speed of the stimulus-response.

In a flash, one second, you're thinking about avoiding plastic bags at the grocery store, and the next, tears spring to your eyes—you're feeling desolate about your beloved dog who died not long enough ago. "What the...?!" you're thinking. "Where did that come from?!?"

Then, you carefully work your way back in your thought process and recognize the connection your mind made in a nanosecond, between plastic bags, and, um, cleaning up after said dog friend.

You think, "Well, that was lame!", but honestly a lot of our so-called gripping, inevitable emotional states start out with a thought that's equally ludicrous. Fortunately, many thoughts like this one can be dismissed with a quick trip back to our common sense.

Let me never give the impression it's not good to feel our emotions or go ahead and let the tears fall when they come. You'll recover much quicker than if you try to hold them in. Just maybe stop and think about what thoughts took you there, and whether you want to take a different fork in the road next time— whether the thought/emotion sequence is helping you get somewhere, or even makes an iota of sense.

More evidence that emotions are given much more importance than biology warrants comes from a startling fact about our nervous system. Apparently, it is so preoccupied with managing the much larger task of running our physical bodies that it can only really register four primitive emotions: happy, sad, calm, and fired up. Everything else, says neuroscientist Lisa Feldman Barret, author of *How Emotions Are Made; the Secret Life of the Brain*, is totally made up in our minds from the unique combination of experiences, conditioning, and personality each of us has.

Because of all these factors in our lives, eventually, we hear a voice in our heads, talking nearly nonstop, making random comments on the passing scene, arguing both sides of a dilemma we're facing, or obsessing over some fear, either rational or irrational.

And, as often as not, we'll respond to those thoughts, the voice in our heads, with emotional responses that may or may not be all that deep and meaningful, it seems.

Well, that's disconcerting. Here I was thinking my drama was pretty darn insightful, important, and real, thank you very much!

The reality is the drama's going to keep happening. It's one of the things that makes us human. And again, not a bad thing, just a cool thing to be aware of, as that awareness opens up a universe of options for us. Think of all the creativity and energy we use to produce all those emotions!

Maybe we could put it to use elsewhere?

This knowledge represents a massive opportunity to declutter our emotions. When we start to think about how much made-up emotion permeates our lives, gets force-fed to us by mass media, along with nearly every fictional story we entertain ourselves with, we see big opportunities for mind clutter that could be cleared out of our lives.

You know, you could be writing the great American novel, learning how to repair drivetrains (mechanics do it; I don't) or even baking a cake from scratch, instead of wringing your mental hands over the stories we make up about almost everything.

It takes some practice, though, so while you contemplate this massive paradigm shift, consider this: If we want to declutter our thoughts and emotions and give ourselves more space and time to realize our goals and ambitions, we have to start somewhere.

So, what should you declutter first?

First, Declutter the Guilts

Guilt: The Gift that Keeps on Giving

If I could inspire you to declutter just one emotion, it would be guilt. **Guilt is truly the emotional clutter gift that keeps on giving.** First, we get to feel bad about the mistakes we make, before, during, and after we make them. Then, every time we remember the action, we feel guilty again.

Did you forget about the misdeed for a little? For shame! Welllllllllll, here's another chance to feel guilty—for not feeling guilty(!), as though we're atoning for our sin by simply holding on to the feeling.

We may even feel guilty when we get in a situation that even remotely reminds of any aspect of our wrong action (trigger).

One of my friends, a true night owl, spoke of feeling guilty about not getting up early in the morning to let the dog out. Usually, his wife simply did it by default while he lay there in bed, feeling guilty, but not moving.

"It felt like I was doing something, at least, by feeling guilty," he said. Sometimes guilt's just a cop-out, a way to feel we're devoting some attention to the "problem," even if no forward motion is happening. Clutter, in other words.

And the guilt feelings can cycle endlessly through our thoughts for years, decades, even a lifetime.

If that weren't enough juice to get out of one misguided action, the more time we spend thinking about the misbehavior (or truly heinous act), the more likely we are to repeat it, in a weak moment (i.e., a moment we're feeling bad about ourselves). With a little dose of guilt, our lives can become cautious and sad, as though we've ruined it once for all.

You really get your money's worth out of guilt!

The "Guilty" Client

I once helped organize the cubicle of an up-and-coming realtor. Her small space was packed to the gills with papers, papers, and more papers. She's all about inspiring people to proactively bring good things into their lives, so we worked diligently to root out all that stress-inducing paper clutter. Since the space was small, it didn't take more than three or four hours.

As I often find, a good 70% of the paper was outdated: expired real estate listings, defunct brochures, superseded forms, and general detritus that was extra-easy to recycle out the door. What struck me was that my client, unlike many I work with, didn't waste one second of our time beating herself up about how it had gotten that way.

She knew my company motto, "non-judgmental organizing," meant no need to apologize for the mess, but more importantly, the urge to feel guilty about it wasn't even on her radar.

By the way—my client? Not long after we cleared her space she moved up to an office of her own at her realty. I like to think I had a hand in that, since her pared down yet personalized cubie looked just like where a successful realtor would work. But the truth is, her own guilt-decluttered mindset is what really did the trick.

Unfortunately, guilt is a hurdle that permeates many of our endeavors, not just in clearing our living/workspaces. With guilt, a little goes a long way, and most of us have WAY more than medically necessary. Decluttering guilt may start slowly and accelerate quickly once we see how good it feels to shed that gratuitous emotion, but we do it by patient repetition.

Self-Compassion: The Better Guilt Buster

According to a University of California, Berkeley study of four hundred participants[7], having compassion for yourself about something you regret doing is significantly more successful in helping you work through and alleviate the guilt. In other words, self-compassion is more effective than simply thinking of yourself as a good person. It seems our soul doesn't simply want a little rah-rah. It wants you to forgive yourself with understanding, to address the situation with some caring, not simply gloss it over. When you practice doing this for yourself, it has the added benefit of helping you be more compassionate with others as well.

Declutter Your Self Criticism: Lighten Up

By the time you're grown, you've probably heard from others an estimated 70,000 times (or was it 150,000 times?), many variations of the following:

"You're wrong."

"That's not the right way."

"Don't do that!"

"That's not good enough."

Etc., ad nauseum.

This is how we learn to criticize ourselves in our habitual thoughts. We didn't come into this world admonishing ourselves from one end of the day to the other. Oh, sure, there's a few overly earnest souls born self-deprecating, but most of us learned

---

[7] Zhang JW, Chen S. Self-Compassion Promotes Personal Improvement From Regret Experiences via Acceptance. Pers Soc Psychol Bull. 2016 Feb;42(2):244-58. doi: 10.1177/0146167215623271. PMID: 26791595.

it from various well-meaning parents, friends, and strangers trying to teach us their version of how to be a human.

Fact is, they may all be well-meaning, but they could also be uninformed and ill-trained. If they were unfortunate enough to be born into unloving homes with no modeling of mutual encouragement, they may unconsciously pass along whatever bad lessons they learned.

We were born almost completely fearless, temperamentally exuberant, calm, loving, and living utterly in the moment. The idea that we're somehow unacceptable is not even a relevant topic to a newborn. We learned to fear the future and feel guilty about the past. Gradually we forgot about living in the present and enjoying it and learned to spend most of our time in the imaginary world in our heads where we are never quite good enough, nor ever quite doing well enough.

But, really, stop and think about it for one minute. As you look around at your co-workers, friends and loved ones, aren't most of them reasonably nice people, generally conscientious about trying to do their best? (Or at least the best they can while constantly hampering themselves with self-disgust.)

The reality is 99.99% of us are in that group, which means that, odds are, you are in that group! In fact, if you're reading this book, I can almost guarantee you are, because you're trying to do things in a better way, which puts you smack in the middle of the kind majority.

Just as we learned to experience a gamut of negative, self-limiting emotions, most of which are mere poppycock, we can all learn, through patience, humor, and gently reminding ourselves over and over, that the present really is not that bad. Truth to tell, it's usually pretty good, even entertaining, and we ourselves are lovely, fine people.

We can similarly learn to banish guilt and fear and self-loathing, with not that much difficult effort, just consistency.

Lightening up on self-criticism is super-important, not only in terms of decluttering, but also in the rest of your life, such as work, relationships, etc., because it's a huge factor in holding you back from being all you can be.

(Kindly) Laugh at Yourself

I commented at a family get-together, "One of the hardest lessons for people to learn is that other people aren't really as interested in our real or imagined shortcomings as we think. Most of the time, they're way too busy obsessing about their own faults to pay much attention to ours."

This family group is far more reasonable, non-judgmental, and willing to laugh gently at themselves in a kind way than the average family, but each had weighed in with their own self-doubt during the visit.

Both members of one couple separately expressed embarrassment for going way over budget on a project recently, and another pair doesn't hesitate to snicker at themselves whenever they feel it's justified. I myself was convinced, several times, that three of the other five people wished me gone because, I assumed, I'm just so eccentric.

On the ride home, the last of the group confessed he just "knew" his grandparents were disgusted with him for staying in a dead-end (but well-paid) job while going to college online, instead of focusing on school. Having tried "broke college student," he had no desire to repeat that.

I just stared in disbelief at this charming young man who had come out of his early-twenties shell and delighted everyone with his wit and conversation, replacing previous habits of silence and mumbling. He could easily have won the "Most Beloved Guest" ribbon that holiday. Actually, I realized, any of the others present could have won it just as handily...

So, then I started laughing, the spell of feeling like "Outcast Number One" was broken, and I made up my mind to get the word I learned out, so here it is: "People, you really don't suck as bad as you think you do." Quit wasting your time berating yourself. And, while you're at it, take a page out of some kindness manual to let your loved ones know you think they're scrumptious!

Declutter Your Embarrassment About Mistakes

Failures Are Just Information

Everyone has heard some version of the old "You can't succeed if you don't make any mistakes, because it means you haven't taken any action" quote. I heard a new twist on the same thought, which blew me away.

"If you think mistakes and failures are bad, you'll never succeed. [Furthermore] multi-millionaires never look at failures as bad, simply as information. Even if they go bankrupt, which many of them do, they still see it as information, not failure." (!)

Hmm...

I am so ticked off! Why didn't someone tell me this before? I could have saved the trouble of beating myself up about five hundred million times! What a lot of wasted hours! Plus, I could have been much further along the road to multi-millionairehood!

We all know there's no percentage in berating a walker-in-training, that is, a one-year-old, every time they fall, or fail to take a designated number of steps forward. In fact, we do the opposite, cheer with enthusiasm at every tiny movement in the right direction, watching the process unfold with the breathless, supportive anticipation of seeing a miracle happen.

Well, it is! What a cornucopia of physical skills and mind-body coordination it takes to get that tiny body to walk, especially with that big, old, out-of-proportion head balanced on top. It's interesting to ponder whether a baby would learn to walk any faster or slower without all that encouragement, but there's absolutely no doubt that continuing to yell at one for not getting it right the first time would have a disastrous effect.

Be Willing to Try, & Acknowledge Your Progress

What about you when you first try your hand at learning to make spreadsheets, or biscuits, or neon sculpture? What if we gave ourselves the same cheering as the 1-year-old gets at every step in the right direction, as well as every wrong guess that we tried, failed, and didn't give up on the process, but kept going till we figured it out?

I never forgot a college friend who said he wished he could learn to play the piano. I asked, "Why don't you?" I knew from my own experience, it can be a step-by-step process that does not take massive natural talent, only the willingness to practice.

He said, as though this made it obvious, "I have friends who go to Juilliard!!" (The well-known performing arts conservatory in New York City.)

I just barely managed to avoid yelling at him: "So! You're telling me, because you can't instantly play as well as the naturally gifted students, who've been playing for years, and who beat out thousands of competitors, to be accepted at this elite college two thousand miles away, that you won't even try?" (We both might have found a home in the drama department, perhaps...)

Few people regret the goofy things they've tried, or the big mistakes they've made, nearly as much as the things they wanted to try and didn't, for whatever reason; too scared, too complacent, too busy, too cluttered.

The most expensive mistake I ever heard of was by a high-level manager in a corporation, who made some ill-fated decision that cost his company ten million dollars. He came to his boss in anguish, saying, "I'll have my letter of resignation on your desk in the morning." The boss said, "What are you talking about? I just spent $10 million on your education! Why would I want to waste that??"

If this brave and thoughtful supervisor could forgive that mistake, do you think you could possibly forgive yourself, for, I don't know, not having walked 5,000 steps by 1 p.m.? Doing your taxes on April 14th, or 20th? Not yet having 6 months of expenses stashed in your savings account? Failing to learn concert-level piano by age 17?

The fact is, in any facet of your life, you're at least one step, to several hundred steps, behind somebody else doing the same thing, in "succeeding" at it. You're also likely several hundred steps ahead of where you started, in any of them.

Shame about your progress, or lack thereof, is irrelevant, unless you've been hired to play at Carnegie Hall and haven't gotten past "Chopsticks." After all, you've been working on a lot of things at once, and probably aren't counting all the dozens of skills you have already long since mastered.

Shame comes from thinking about the things you wish you hadn't done in the past, too: unkind acts, thefts on some level, lots and lots of lies, etc. If you feel bad about them, congratulate yourself for being a person who cares, realize you've grown and are much less likely to do them in the future. Put the shame to rest. Not one single person is immune.

Declutter Your Judgmental Thoughts of Others

If self-criticism takes up a big part of our waking hours, there's a good chance we're also dishing on many others in our lives, whether friend, foe, or stranger. It's hard to say which is the most destructive and the biggest waste of time.

Sometimes it's hard to resist, especially when that other is currently acting like a total jerk, or worse, to you.

That old line about not judging me till you've walked a mile in my shoes is the one to tattoo on the inside of your left eyelid; "Take it easy on yourself," is the one you can ink on your right. That's the kicker when it comes to judging other people—you really don't know what they've been through that makes them act crazy.

There's Always a Reason

Years ago, at the engineering company I worked at, one of the drafters, whose work had been acceptable, if not stellar, started taking a slow descent into the unacceptable. Most everyone in our small company was up in arms, complaining loudly about the outrage of his declining performance. (Engineers tend to be extra-focused, to put it politely, on things being done perfectly, you may be reassured to know.) However, something told me to stick to one of my favorite guidelines, "There's always a reason (why people act the weird ways that they do)," and reserve judgment.

Not long after, he left the company, or may have been fired, I don't remember. We heard from him several months later when he called to say he was in treatment for severe gout, a product of having been exposed to Agent Orange while serving in Vietnam. This had been the cause of his problem!

35

It takes a while to train yourself to resist the temptation to judge others, but it's so, so worth it, not only in terms of time savings, but also stress relief. Running the world in your mind is just so tiring! Besides, if you're spiritually inclined, you could always just say, "It's God's job to judge. Not mine." Delegate that!

Decluttering judgmental thoughts is a process which, luckily, most of us get better at as we get older. I pretty much knew everything, including how everyone should act, in my early twenties, and over the years, I've gotten a lot less sure of myself on all that, to my great benefit. Now if someone cuts me off in traffic, I assume they're late for their doctor appointment, instead of assuming they're complete ___holes. If they honk loudly at me, I just exclaim, as my young pal Matt Van Essen once taught me, "It could be an old friend!"

If a clerk is rude, I assume she's having a bad day, not that I am now. This was one the hardest skills for me to learn. I spent my childhood often being berated for being "too sensitive" (i.e., thin-skinned). I got my feelings hurt at the drop of a hat. I was in my twenties before I realized being sensitive could be a good thing.

Declutter Your Rugged Individualism ("Don't Help Me!")

For the past thirty years, I've spent time with people addicted to a variety of things, including work. They've all been some of the smartest people I've ever met. And guess what? They all had dismal childhoods, from which they learned early on to be totally self-sufficient and not accept or ask for help from anyone.

"Cigarettes are my friends!" they may say, laughing, but deep down, they mean it. Cigarettes are what they feel they can count on, not people.

The nuclear family, isolated from extended family, may lose out on this one; it doesn't always have the advantage of solid life wisdom and experience from older loved ones. If this is you, don't hesitate to reach out to family or friends for life hacks. Sometimes even a tidbit of insight makes all the difference.

Over-independence hits us hard in the economic side of life, too. Small business expert Chuck Blakeman, author of *Making Money is Killing Your Business* and *Employees Are Always a Bad Idea,* scoffs at the American obsession with rugged individualism. He says it's the best way to fail at business, either by keeping profits low or your free time at a minimum.

On the flip side are the superstars of life who've learned to focus all their work on the one thing they do best and delegate everything else. This means they must ask for help, and they get very rich doing it.

The Colorado real estate world was shown that for many years, with one northern Colorado realtor doing the single task he excelled at and enjoyed most: meeting clients to list their properties. He was so astonishingly good at it that his only job was to take two listing appointments a day (set up for him by others), one in the morning and one in the afternoon, Monday through Friday, for years.

Every other aspect of the transactions, from scheduling inspections to arranging financing, to managing the marketing, to handling counteroffers, to setting up closings, was taken care of by others. With this system, the realtor and his team provided livelihoods for over a dozen people. Eventually he retired from active real estate to teach others his system.

Not going to lie—I myself lean toward the overly independent side.

If I had back all the hours I've spent beating my brains out to figure out some tricky engineering solution on my own, instead of asking for help from the client, the "City," the contractor, the colleague, or whoever, I could have made 17 quilts by now! (If I quilted, that is, but you get the idea.)

And I didn't even have a dismal childhood, per se, just a lot of moving, as I mentioned earlier, which taught me to rely solely on myself.

If your friend is an addict of some kind, especially if they're addicted to rugged individualism, encourage them to allow you to assist them from time to time; if you yourself are the one stuck on stubborn independence, this is one load of baggage it's good to lose.

Find small, non-scary ways to reach out and trust your future staff. We need your brilliance, and you may appreciate the money!

The Practice of Mental and Emotional Decluttering

This section covers ideas for how to clear mental clutter, from the simplest to the most complex. They can be used to clear out your resistance to decluttering your possessions, or for any area of your life that's bothering you.

Since we are all individuals, some techniques will appeal to us more than others. And, just as individual bodies are unique in how they respond to different nutrients, our emotional make-up is just as unique. Some are not bothered by much of anything; others are very sensitive and affected more deeply by emotions. Don't criticize yourself if you are at the emotional end of the spectrum. Simply find a few techniques that work for you and put them to work when you feel overwhelmed.

The Power of Awareness

Sometimes it's enough to just become aware of some of our roadblocks, and with humor and patience, talk ourselves into a better course of action: "Yes, I realize I became desperately afraid to take out the trash after Dad fell on the ice taking it out one day. He broke his leg, but I can make a different choice. I can proceed more cautiously and avoid those smells without breaking any bones."

When we're in the grips of some emotional storm, it's hard to realize that it will pass of its own accord, just as it has all these thousands of times before, or else you wouldn't be calmly reading this, would you?

This sounds like a quick and sort of empty suggestion, but it's truly huge. Even though it almost never feels like it will ever end or get better when we're in emotional turmoil, it really, really does, close to 100% of the time. One of the benefits of getting older is that occasionally, we remember that fact!

You can even decide on your own to drop it (also huge). Entire books and healing methods have been based on this one idea (Check out the Sedona Method, discussed further below, for one.)

Or you can look to someone you admire for their calmness, or whatever quality, to see that it is truly possible. I use this technique when I haven't flown in a while, and that old fear comes whooshing back. I keep my eyes pinned on the flight attendants and think, "These heroes fearlessly do this every day, and see how devil-may-care they look! Maybe I can bravely hang in there for 3-5 hours a year?" I once complimented a flight attendant for serenely paging through a magazine throughout a steadily bumpy flight. She said, "I actually prefer it this way. Then no one bothers me."

Talk to Friends (But Be Selective!)

Telling your troubles to an empathic listener—i.e., one who doesn't argue with you and tell you that you don't have any reason to feel that way, for Pete's sake!—actually causes a chemical change in our bodies that relieves depression.

Talk therapy can range from two buddies sharing a couple of beers and conversation, to engaging a professional counselor. It works by boosting your self-esteem and giving you a chance to see things from a more relaxed perspective via another person's supportive eyes.

With friends you have to pick and choose who to spill your guts to. They may have their own issues that weigh heavily on their "advice." An old friend of mine never had a good word to say about any of the men in my life as soon as he heard any report of their less-than-enjoyable behavior. He would instantly start trying to talk me into breaking up with them. I found myself trying desperately to regain my friend's approval of these guys, most of whom he never met, after I had made the mistake of candidly reporting in.

He himself did not have a close romantic relationship (and hadn't for years), which should have given me a clue, but the penny didn't drop till one day he made a comment about himself with respect to his ex-wife that made him sound like a complete jerk (but which was totally inaccurate). Finally, I realized that all his negative comments about my men friends had little to do with the friends themselves and everything to do with his own poor opinion of himself. "Projecting" is what the pros call it.

Another pal of mine has three friends on speed dial, each of whom she must call after any (dependably downer) conversation with her mom just to stay upright. Problem solved! Though there might be some more proactive solutions, eh?

Meditation

There are dozens of different ways people like to meditate, from sitting in utter silence in a certain seated posture, moving as little as possible and doggedly attempting to rid the mind of all thoughts (that part is close to impossible, so don't berate yourself if you find it an insurmountable challenge), to listening to music, to meditations guided by the voices by others. Even though some people will tell you their way is the "only" way to meditate, don't believe them.

"Sitting just quietly," as Ferdinand the Bull loved to do in the much-beloved children's story of the same name, works as well, though other delicious feelings show up with some of the more advanced meditation techniques.

Meditation seems deceptively simple, yet the benefits that build up over time with regular practice are astonishing and have been scientifically documented.[8] Stress relief, self-awareness, focus, and greater happiness can result from meditating for even just ten minutes a day.

My own twist on meditation is to smile slightly throughout (when I remember to, that is). It's nearly impossible to drift into the dark side of depression when we're smiling. Better ideas come to us when we are happy and relaxed, versus wallowing in fear, because again, then the lizard brain rules. I figure it can't hurt meditation outcomes either.

(Not to mention that slight smiles do not cause wrinkles, but they do build facial muscles to resist the making of other wrinkles. Bonus!)

Sit Quietly, Do Nothing

Taking the idea of "sitting just quietly" one step further, we come to the most decluttered meditation of all: Sit quietly and do absolutely nothing! Neither think, nor plan, nor pray, nor

---

[8] https://www.nccih.nih.gov/health/meditation-in-depth

meditate. Look out a window, stare at a wall, let yourself become bored with yourself. I was told, "Do this for 10 minutes a day, and your life will change dramatically in thirty days."

I have been doing this one for a few months and can't believe the amazingly useful thoughts that have shown up in my mind. It could be a completely new way of looking at something or a reminder of a super-important task I had all but forgotten about. Sometimes I find my focus shifting from what I thought was "the main thing right now" to something completely different, and realizing it has higher priority in moving my plans forward. This practice brings you back to the present moment, which is usually much more manageable than the fears milling around about the past or the future.

They say you're listening to your soul or higher self when you do this practice, which is why it's so profound. Your soul/higher self knows what it's doing! I started writing a quick note of the ten-minute thoughts each day, to remind myself of those brilliant insights.

I can only assume that part of what happens in these quiet meditations is a chance to hear our own intuition, a vastly underrated faculty we all have but may have been trained to ignore. (If you've ever thought of someone out of the blue, only to have that person call you within a few minutes, you've experienced intuition. If you've "had a hunch" about something, that's also intuition.)

It often comes to us with valuable info, which may sound like the obvious conclusion or like common sense, but since it sounds like our own voice, we don't know whether to trust it. Do trust it. You are wiser than you know.

There are those who find meditation allows them to connect with the Sacred (God, Creator, "the Higher," however they see the Divine), which makes it that much more compelling, peace-creating, and joyful!

Journaling

Moving up the spectrum of involvement we come to journaling, which, word on the street is, actually releases that same stress-relieving chemical reaction that talking with friends (or counselors) does. (Endorphins again.)

Journaling doesn't have to be complicated. Even a humble spiral notebook can be used, though it is a good excuse to use up some of those enticing blank books you've purchased in the past, never again to write a word in. Some people journal throughout their lives, while others only do it when they're in crisis mode.

A good technique I've used with success when stress was high is to write whatever pours out of you, no matter how nonsensical it may seem, once a day, enough to fill up three pages. You may end up tossing it after things resolve themselves, not only to let go of those bad memories, but just the fact that little of it may be usable for anything later. It is rather astonishing how stress-relieving this practice can be. If three pages takes too long, try one page.

Counseling

If your past has been more traumatic than average, or you simply don't want to talk with your friends about it, counseling can be extremely effective in helping you leave the past behind and move forward in your life.

This is true especially if their practice leans toward "solution-oriented counseling." They may discuss with you some of what in your past contributed to your troubles of today. But they don't endlessly revisit those past events and emotions. (For many people, not only is it not helpful to keep going over old events, it may, in fact, prolong their misery.) Instead, these counselors focus on what changes you could make in your life, and what habits you could develop that to get you closer to where you want to go and make the outcome more likely.

Counseling often teaches us to be gentle with ourselves, which most all of us could use. In counseling, we can learn new techniques that help us get around or dissolve our own emotional blocks.

Energy Healing

What makes clearing emotional clutter extra challenging is that our emotions are tied up with our physical bodies as well. The West has awoken to what the East has known for thousands of years: our minds and bodies are inextricably intertwined; what happens to one impacts the other.

We've had an inkling with some of our expressions, like "having a gut feeling," a "sinking feeling in our stomachs," feeling "broken-hearted," or having the "guts to go for it." But we have not consistently made the connection that our emotions live all over our bodies, not just in our heads.

If you've been journaling or using other low-tech methods for years and still feel your emotions holding you back from all you'd like your life to be, my own experience has taught me that doing some sort of energy healing work is one of the biggest time savers of all.

Why is that? Remember the old model of an atom, with the neutrons, protons, and electrons? Physicists used to think mass was made up of these atoms with the bigger protons and neutrons in the middle, and the tinier electrons whirling around the outside in predictable orbits. Then they decided those particles were, in fact, made up of smaller particles called quarks, which were themselves whirling madly around each other to give the illusion of bigger mass.

Now quantum physics speaks instead of "energy bundles" which have no mass at all, just a lot of empty space (over 99% to be exact) and highly condensed energy, creating atoms which pop in and out of existence. So, that's pretty hard to wrap your mind around, but consider this:

Most of us can recall the theory of relativity from high school science ($E = mc^2$), right? Looking straight at the math equation of this, we might notice that the amount of energy in our bodies is roughly our weight times the speed of light times the speed of light. No matter your weight, this is a very, very big number!

Call me crazy, but it's not that big a leap to see why energy healing could be so powerful, since emotions strongly impact the energy of our bodies.

If the idea of energy healing has you a little panicked or uncertain, fear not. It ranges from practices as simple as taking three deep slow breaths in a row (instant calm-down, at least a little), to meditation, to any number of DIY techniques, to those that experienced practitioners help you with. Acupuncture, which has become much more widely accepted in the West in recent years, is an energy-healing technique.

You could also simply call them mind-body methods and remove all the eccentric-sounding terms in one.

At their core, these practices all do two basic things: they remove emotional blocks tied up in your body and nervous system, and they help you get in touch with your inner person (who is always a being of goodness, no matter how much of a turkey/jerk you are acting like on the outside).

It might seem odd that an engineer would be checking out these "alternative" practices, but at heart, I'm a practical and cut-to-the-chase kind of person. As they say, "If it's stupid, but it works, then it isn't stupid!"

Emotional Freedom Technique (Tapping)

An extremely effective energy healing technique you can learn to use all by yourself is called the Emotional Freedom Technique, or EFT. Also called "tapping," EFT has become widely popular in recent years for its simplicity and power to heal emotional blocks quickly.[9] It involves lightly tapping a series of nine or more locations around the face and upper body. These points are located at the endpoints of the energy channels in the body used by acupuncturists (meridians).

While tapping in a regular fashion through these points and talking about, or even simply thinking about a particular issue in your life that's holding you back, from a physical pain to an emotional rut you keep falling into, you release stuck energy, and often feel an immediate relief in as short as a few minutes.

Not only can you use it to defuse the emotional hang-ups, but you can also relieve symptoms from chronic and acute illnesses, and physical pain. (As a bonus you are likely to feel a rush of those neurotransmitters mentioned earlier, endorphins, which is a big part of the immediate sensation of feeling better.)

You might tap on an issue for five to ten minutes, then check back in to see how you feel about the issue or pain. Sometimes the improvement is very slight in one tapping session (still a good thing) and sometimes it's extensive. Another idea about the issue or pain may pop into your mind, and you can tap on that side of it, or simply repeat the process a few more times, as long as you continue to feel improvement that day.

---

[9] See https://tappingsolution.s3.amazonaws.com/APP/Marketing/TS-Science-Data-Research.pdf for a compendium of 36 research studies on EFT.

While using tapping for an emotional sticking point in your life, the method seems laughably counter-intuitive; you often begin by talking about it while tapping, with all the most extreme negativity you can drum up. Most Americans are shocked by this, as we've been advised for decades to "always speak positively" about ourselves and our lives.

However, the fact is "what you resist persists," so as you are valiantly resisting the urge to say those revolting opinions out loud, you are actually holding onto them even more tightly in your nervous system!

The tapping technique is a true mind-body release because it scrambles that negative programming we've subconsciously applied to ourselves. Tapping allows us to genuinely let it go instead of fooling ourselves into thinking we have. Oddly enough, the more emotion you put into the negative side, the more deeply it is cleared.

Even after many years of successful experience with tapping, I am still shocked by how well it works. Recently, I was *so upset* about something (SO upset!). I started walking around a loop from my house that takes about ten minutes to finish. Since no one was around, I threw myself into it, walking and sobbing, tapping angrily and close to yelling about how upset I was, and how "Tapping is NOT going to work this time, because I am just SO upset!" About three houses away from returning to my own, it dawned on me: "Oh...I actually do feel better. Hmm." I wasn't quite ready to laugh about it, but I had to admit it I had almost forgotten what I was so upset about. I had already moved on to thinking about something else, and I definitely felt better.

After you have tapped for a few minutes on the negative side of the issue, you can continue to tap while talking about a positive outcome you'd like to replace it with. This step isn't always necessary. Sometimes simply tapping on the negative has a beneficial effect.

At its root, EFT works by calming down the amygdala (fight-or-flight center of the brain) so we can engage the thinking parts of our brains again and start to see creative solutions to our dilemmas.

There are hundreds of instructional videos and other information on the internet for help with tapping. One of the best websites is https://www.thetappingsolution.com which is hosted by the Ortner family. Although they did not develop the method, they have done much to publicize and explore ways to use EFT. Each year in early March they put together a "Tapping Summit," compiling dozens of hours of instructional videos on all the different ways tapping can assist in our lives. They include interviews with experts and various tapping sequences. Access to the summit is free for a few days, then can be purchased for a modest fee to use indefinitely.

(One caveat about tapping is that, though it is effective for most of us for most situations, when a person has experienced deep trauma in their lives, the release tapping brings can be retraumatizing, and is better worked through only with the help of a licensed EFT practitioner, at least until the trauma has been defused.)

(See also the Additional Resources section for further information on EFT.)

Neuro-Emotional Technique

Neuro-Emotional Technique (NET) is based on the same energy system of the body that acupuncture is, the meridians designated by Chinese medicine. It is performed by practitioners who've taken extensive training. Many chiropractors include NET as part of their practice.

NET is designed to get rid of emotional wounds that are stored in our bodies, in just a few minutes. Some of these wounds go away with one treatment, while others take a few treatments due to the old "layers-of-an-onion" phenomenon, which is when the clearing one emotional block reveals yet another hidden underneath. It helps to work with a practitioner, as they are trained to get to the root of the issue very quickly. I had some very old resistances and rebellions simmering in my psyche that talking to myself hadn't ousted, mainly because I had no idea what they were, till my chiropractor and I rooted them out.

NET is readily available in most cities. See: https://www.netmindbody.com/find-a-practitioner/ for a directory of practitioners.

There are many other excellent energy-healing techniques for eliminating stubborn emotional blocks, including Reiki, the Sedona Method, Spiritual Response Therapy (SRT), the Yuen method (Chinese Energetic Medicine), and many others. These are less familiar to most Americans, but each has a particular approach to energy healing, and different techniques appeal to different people.

Some techniques can be learned in classes and practiced by yourself, and others are more effective with an experienced practitioner. Many of the methods have directories of practitioners, and you may be able to get a good recommendation by inquiring at a health food store or asking an integrated medical practitioner for a referral.

The Sedona Method deserves special mention. Even though it is technically an energy healing technique, it feels more mental, as it's done by voluntarily letting go of an emotional response through words and your imagination, much as you would open your fingers to let go of a pencil you're holding.

I first tried it from a 15-minute introduction the night before I took a plane trip that I was very apprehensive about. I repeatedly imagined releasing the fear down and out of my body, feeling like a complete fool. It was more like forcing it down with a steam roller instead of gently dropping a pencil. However, the next day I made it through the dreaded take-off with only a fraction of my former fear and I haven't been afraid to fly since.

Acupuncture is an effective energy healing technique with a decidedly physical component, which is only performed by highly trained experts. (By the way, acupuncture is recognized by the World Health Organization as being beneficial for over two dozen conditions, and the U.S. military routinely uses it for pain relief, including battlefield injuries.)

I've tried all these techniques and more, partly for myself, and partly in the spirit of inquiry for future clients who might need something similar. They've all been helpful!

A Note of Caution

Don't get caught up in endlessly searching for the next wonderful energy healing technique, thinking "Maybe I haven't found the right one yet, since the last one didn't solve everything!"

This leads to its own kind of anxiety, not much different than shopping envy, and becomes another kind of clutter.

The bottom line is they all do somewhat the same thing. They all shift energy—but from many different approaches. Instead of leaping from one to the next, better to find one or two energy-healing techniques that make sense to you and delve into them more deeply than fritter away a lot of years looking for the ideal one.

* * *

Now that you've cleared out some of those emotional blocks and unhelpful emotions, what positive emotions could you replace them with?

Gratitude – Remember Your Blessings

Gratitude may be one of the best ways to pull yourself out of a funk. Researchers who study brainwaves emitted during emotions say gratitude is one of the highest vibrational frequency attitudes we produce.

And that's a good thing. Without going into a lot of excruciating biology, just think: higher frequency emotions = closer to blissed out!

Those who purposely apply gratitude in daily life say listing things you are grateful for is one of the fastest ways to improve your mood in an instant, no matter how grudgingly you start the list.

A gratitude journal helps encourage the practice of gratitude. Begin by listing at least five things each day you are grateful for (to play the game right, they ought to be five new things every day, not simply the same-old, same-old).

This gets you in the habit of looking for new, joyful details each day, and before long, brings you to the realization that there are more "good" things in life than "bad." And they're not that far below the surface; they're easy to see once you start looking for them.

1,000 Minutes

You can start with something as simple as feeling grateful for the minutes in the day. "What are you talking about, Chiquita?! Whoever has enough minutes in the day??" The habit of thinking we never have enough time is well-ingrained in most of us, however, the arithmetical truth is that, after subtracting out time for sleeping, we are each gifted for free with about 1,000 minutes every day.

What? That's crazy! Where does it all go? Not going to lie; it takes time to take care of the bod all day long. And great handfuls of time also get frittered in these very emotional drains we've been discussing. But even with all that stuff burning up daylight, we could still, perhaps, see ourselves achieving something meaningful, or storing up a joyful experience to treasure, in 1,000 minutes, eh?

The gift of those minutes was brought home to me a few years ago, along a stretch of highway in Brighton, Colorado, where the speed limit abruptly changes from 65 mph to stoplight. I slowed and stopped for the yellow-to-red light, dubiously noting the tanker truck traveling a little too close for comfort behind me and having time only to mentally cross my fingers.

In a second the trucker swerved around me into the left turn lane, ran through the red light, crossed the intersection, and continued down the road. I didn't even have time to be scared, and my life could have been over. Later, I was grateful the trucker was a good enough driver to make the dodge, since he or she clearly wasn't going to stop for the light. Later still, I was even more grateful when I realized the situation turned out perfectly. Had I slowed but continued on through the light, the trucker would likely have plowed into me, with no room to go around.

Small Joys

There are a zillion other things to be grateful for as well. One key is to look for the tiniest joy, rather than thinking you need to hold out for something quite significant; don't wait for the once-in-five-years promotion to be grateful, while missing the daily funny antics of someone's pet. Be grateful for the smell of baking bread in the sub shop/convenience store instead of waiting for your kid to graduate.

Two reasons for that. Noticing the small daily joys adds immensely to the enjoyment of your life, as well as keeping you in a more relaxed frame of mind, open for wonderful solutions to life's problems to wander into that mind. And, the reality is, not only do we forget to celebrate our big wins in an extended way (as in, "Oh, yeah, that 'big dream' got realized yesterday didn't it?") we just forget about them all together, in the minutiae of daily life. Waiting to feel happy till something's "really worth it" leaves us not happy very often.

Happiness takes practice!

Gratitude – Simplify Your Affirmations

As I'm one of those people who has spent longish spans of time pondering the meaning of life and the nature of God, you can bet I was once stumped about how to approach the practice of affirmations/prayer.

Is it best to pray for everything you want, relying on God for all things (with taking the appropriate God-directed action, of course)?

Ask just once? Ask over and over?

Ask only for the "big stuff," and don't bother God with the small matters?

Ask only in the correct format (If you put the money in the right way, you'll get what you want? God as Divine Vending Machine?) Hmm...

Then there's the advice from approximately every self-help book known to humankind: State your affirmations (what you want to happen) in the present tense as though you already have it, such as "I earn $122,000 a year," then let God/the Universe bring it to you. And, of course, you'll take the actions your intuition senses He/She/It is strongly suggesting to you.

What kicks this one in the rear is the tiny voice in your head saying "Ha! No, you don't! Fool!"

How happy I was to find this excellent middle ground. The seeker advised the best way to handle the situation: Say "Thank you, God, for the success in my life."

"Bingo!" I thought. It covers all the bases. It gets you into gratitude mode, which everybody says is the way to go. And, we've all had at least some success in life, so we don't have to feel like liars.

Wanting to leave no stone unturned, I extrapolated, adding a couple more: "Thank you, God, for the love in my life," and "Thank you, God, for the abundance in my life."

Simple template, and, not only have all those things started going better for me, but I get a little endorphin rush (buzz) every time I say one of them, so I've got instant access to free bliss-on-demand.

This is a double bonus point. Not only do you simplify your spiritual life, but you also declutter some major fretting about "doing it right." (This is another short sentence which, nevertheless, has vast implications for improving your life.)

Now I've reached another plateau, having come to believe God & Associates are much more willing to come to our assistance than generally thought, just as any good parents would do for their children. The key is to ask.

By the way, clearing blocks to affirmations is an excellent way to use EFT (tapping). You simply tap on each argument your brain comes up with against your affirmation, and eventually those arguments melt away. The affirmation becomes something both you and your body can believe in. It puts you in a better position to receive all those blessings God is trying to give you!

Appreciate Everything

Sometimes when everyone's grumpy, or sad, or afraid, and life seems dismal and you can't catch a break, it's hard to feel gratitude. Platitudes don't help much in this situation; nor does it help to know in our head the fact that we're likely living in our head—primarily imagining it will never get any better.

"Yes, and please don't tell me I can't appreciate the "good" without experiencing the "bad," or I will kick you!"

Sorry, I am going to tell you that, because it's true. Never is anyone more grateful for the joy of happy, relaxed toes, than when the stubbed one finally stops hurting. A few fast-food meals in a row, and a ripe peach to eat seems heavenly. If your whole house feels like the "before" picture in a makeover show, think of how much richer the delight in any improvement you can make in it!

Sometimes we can't appreciate the "ugly" in our lives, but if we're lucky or very wise, we may be able to remember a time when that circumstance that broke our heart at the moment became a surprise blessing as it eventually unfolded. The lost sweetheart we later realized when we met again was not a good match for us at all. An irritating minor car accident a young man and woman had that later turned into a joyful marriage. Unable to purchase a house that seemed "perfect" for your family due to structural problems being discovered, only to find another house three times more dazzling, and still in your price range! (All true stories.) There's a million of them, am I right?

There's always the good old tried and true. For a moment contrast your situation to any of a billion or more situations in the world where people may never have enough to eat, much less be able to read these words, or others who would love to be able to use their limbs. No guilt trip intended, simply some perspective that can accelerate your return to gratitude.

When the everyday glumnesses get you down, it usually works to take that blank ten minutes described in the meditation section. It's all about becoming completely present, at which point it may be the work of on instant to find some tiny detail in your surroundings that delights you with its beauty, to think of how the cute antics of a toddler of your acquaintance that always make you chuckle, or simply breathe easily and notice how peaceful that makes you feel.

Thanks for the Ickiness!

The most extreme take on the "not resisting that which you dislike" came to me only in the last few days, proving again sometimes it does pay to delay. The unorthodox recommendation was to express thanks for the unwelcome circumstance. "Thank you for these unaffordable car repairs." "Thank you for how mad I am at life." "Thank you for the promotion I didn't get after all." According to the method, you don't even have to believe the gratitude you are expressing for these nasty circumstances, but the energy around the situation will change, and you find wonderful new ideas and resources to help to solve the problem will arise, or you will be blessed with healing.

This is a testament to how much energy is bound up in arguing with what is in life, and how valuable it is to state what's bugging you rather than let it circle endlessly around your psyche in an attempt to make it go away by ignoring it. The relief from acknowledging it frees up your creativity to deal with it.

(If all else fails, forgive what you can't appreciate. Forgiveness is always for your benefit, much more than for the forgiv-ee's, so take advantage of that fact.)

Altruism

Doing something nice or giving something nice to other people is one of life's biggest natural rushes. I think it might even top gratitude for bringing your mood instantly from misery into the glorious zone, primarily because it's active, and we humans like to take action!

Except for the most hard-hearted, nothing brings you out of yourself and into the present moment faster than focusing on someone else's needs. It blesses both of you since you get to be in the position of being able to give. We all love to be the hero.

The only danger is going overboard with your altruism, always giving, to the point of depleting your own resources, or trying to "fix" people with help they didn't ask for.

We've probably heard thousands of times, "It's more blessed to give than receive." I was brought up short when someone asked, "Is that really true?"

As it turns out, both giving and receiving are blessed. If you're fixed on giving and never allowing yourself to receive, then you deny the others in your life the joy of giving to you. And being the hero part of the time...Let them!

What if you are too far removed from the situation to give any practical help in a timely fashion? You can at least send them love, light, and blessings from your heart. The more you learn about human energy and how messages are transmitted from one to the other through no logical channels (recalling the "intuition" reference a few pages back) the more you will see this is a valid helpful activity. An added benefit is that the love and light you send out to others also slides through your own energy field, giving you a sweet dose as well!

Sucks to Be You

On the flip side, if you are really struggling to bring up any compassion for somebody getting themselves into a pickle through their own dopey actions, you can at least think to yourself, "Wow! Sucks to be you," and/or "Bless your heart!" with a smidgen of kindness in your own heart. This is what I do in the face of people whining over nothing and throwing a fit in which they blame everyone else for their problems. It's a big improvement over what I used to do, which was trying to appease them. The kindness is in not saying these two magic phrases out loud.

Now we turn to the next brave stage in emotional decluttering: replacing negative emotions with positive ones by plain, old choice. In other words, "Hey, energy healing is great, but let's not forget the simplest of all—"

Attitude Adjustment – Self-Appreciation Society

Here's a quick way to replace some negative emotion with attitude adjustment. I've demonstrated how this technique is done with my favorite emotion, guilt, but you could just as easily substitute your own fave, such as anger, fear, dread, or whatever. Simply fill in the blank. Here goes:

1. You're amazing! Wow! Have you looked at all you're doing these days? Managing a career, keeping family, friends, and your accountant happy, exercising, running a home, balancing your diet, retirement planning, answering emails, volunteering, taking time for spiritual refreshment, getting enough ice cream, recycling, resting, and recreationing. No wonder life can feel overwhelming

sometimes (and guilt-worthy) if we don't keep up with it all.

Well, forget that! I hate to say "should" since it's a word that can short-circuit straight to [guilt], but you "have the option to" feel impressed by yourself for juggling all that. How's that for re-framing?

It is very impressive, all that you do.

And don't even think about adding in any extra [guilt] for not also baking cupcakes for the class party, running for state senator, and keeping the car maintenance records up to date!

2. Consider that the [guilt] might be someone else's; it's a habit we learn growing up, listening to our well-meaning, but sometimes overzealous, mentors teaching us how to be "good" human beings. Their version of "good" may have been a valuable, beneficial one, but it could also include a heavy dose of their own fears and misguided training. When you're a kid, you may or may not question their version of life, unless you're a born rebel. Eventually their edicts become ingrained in your head, whispering the proclamations back at you at any moment, opportune or not.

I'm still pondering how I feel about continuing relationships with older relatives who verbally abuse us or, in their version, "warn us out of love," but there's no question about what to say to the mom who lives in our head: "Do you think this is this really helping me, Mom, or does it even have anything to do with me? If you think it's that important, can you find a more respectful, kind, or non-mocking way to say it?"

3. [Guilt] takes up SO much time, with very little payout except tied hands, queasy stomachs, stalled-out dreams, and so forth. So, enough of that; good reason to delete.

As with so many things in life, dismal emotions can arise when we forget:

A. How amazing we are, and
B. That making mistakes is one of the prime ways we learn and grow as people.

Inspire Yourself – Create Your Own "Ten Commandments"

In his luminous book, *The Rod Effect: Master 8 Philosophies That Took me from the Projects to NFL Super Bowl Stardom,* my friend and former business trainer, Rod Smith (yes, that Rod Smith, of Denver Bronco fame) wrote, "Make sure you understand the power of words." He was talking about speaking to yourself and others about your dreams for the future, and the power of doing that in a positive way to help bring them about.

He also said, "Write some of your favorite scriptures down in your own words, so they will create an emotional, personal connection with those biblical words. You will feel amazing every time you speak [them]."

I went one step further and created my own Ten Commandments. These are not in any way meant to replace the original Ten! A better term might be "Your Top Ten Trademark Slogans." They are simply the top ten words or phrases that never fail to fire you up (or calm you down, if need be) with the wisdom that speaks uniquely to you. After threatening to for years, I finally had mine printed up as small posters and am astonished at how compelling it is to look at them in big print several times a day.

My favorite one is "Quarterly Allowance," in honor of what I was once taught: that you don't need to have one or more million dollars in the bank to be considered "independently wealthy," you only need to have enough passive income coming in, whether from stock dividends, royalties, rent, or whatever, to pay your basic bills! This gives you a lot of free time, which you could use to follow up on other money-making projects that could move you from "basic independent wealth" to "lush budget independent wealth."

It also cracks me up every time I see it. The words remind me of many books I've read by English humorist P.G. Wodehouse, which featured a lot of trust fund babies. These characters were always a little nervous about keeping their trust fund manager (usually a rich uncle) happy, so those Quarterly Allowances would keep coming down the pike...

I told you about my friend Matt Van Essen's inspired comment "It could be an old friend!" when a fellow driver honked his disapproval at my being in his way. That's another of my Top Ten. It inspires me not to take other people's bad moods too seriously.

The very top of my list, however, goes to a phrase given to me by an acquaintance of mine with quite a checkered past. Through my own ignorance I had gotten myself in a situation, such that answering the door could lead to very unpleasant consequences. It was useless, too, to answer the door in this instance, as I had no way of solving the situation. Having much experience in this type of dilemma, he said "There's no law that says you have to answer the door, no matter who's knocking. You just have to hold your nerve!"

That phrase "Hold your nerve" sizzled through me like lightning and spoke to my timid soul in no uncertain terms! "I'm keeping that one!" I yelled to myself, for whenever I need a dose of courage. (I use it a lot.)

(Also, small, but mighty, the single word "Magician" hangs over the door to my office. Works, well, like magic, for those days when I'm not feeling it.)

Slow Down! – Declutter Your Busyness

"If you remain in a perpetual state of busyness, and are always preoccupied in survival emotions, you never actually have the opportunity to believe in yourself."

—*Joe Dispenza*

A pervasive form of emotional clutter in our lives is the tendency to fill every waking moment with activity, noise, or commitments. Americans especially are hooked into the idea that "There are things that need doing, therefore we need to be doing something at all times to get those things done."

Add to that the exuberant human tendency to take on far more projects than we can complete in a lifetime, much less in the next two months, and you have some real opportunities for overwhelm.

At one time in my life I worked nearly full-time as an engineer, raised and shuttled around two lively little boys, one of which had a restricted diet for several years, did most of the housework for our large house, cooked (with a low skill levels on those last two, I can tell you), wrote books and peddled educational toys for extra money, hosted an exercise class for a friend at my house once a week, cleaned up after the dog, and attempted to grow some flowers (One too many things. The flowers didn't make it.)

There were many times that I did not dare sit down, or I would never have gotten up again. And I wasn't very cheerful a lot of the time. There were a lot of sweet moments with my boys that I had no energy to appreciate, and that's a big regret. Thank goodness for grandparents, who take the time!

I realize this scenario has been played out millions of times in homes all over America and the world. A lot of where it comes from is fear-based, fear of not enough income, of not being considered a good enough spouse and parent, of messing up the child-raising, the constant fear for their well-being. It keeps us scrambling to keep up with an impossible schedule.

If only I had known about the amygdala back then! If only I had known how much meditation helped! If only I'd had a cook and a housekeeper!

The funny thing is, the most time-consuming of those activities are long gone out of my life. I have streamlined my life to the bare bones, and I still sometimes feel like I have too much to do. So that's lesson Number 1. Realize it never really goes away unless you get proactive about decluttering your busyness. It's far too easy to fill up all your time with commitments that can get in the way of enjoying the now.

To-Do List Heresy from the Pulpit!

Some years ago, the minister at a church I attended did a series on decluttering; the overall premise being that clutter of all kinds distracts us from a relationship with God. He even quoted some Biblical scriptures in support of the idea. I thought, "Great! This is outstanding! Even God—or at least the Bible—supports decluttering!"

It was when he turned to the subject of To-Do Lists that I faltered. He said, "Whenever I start feeling too stressed and overwhelmed, I lop off about 75% of my to-do list."

"What?" I thought. "How can you just do that? Isn't that, like, illegal? What about all those little 'A's, 'B's, and 'C's on the priority list? Those 'C's that turn into emergencies if we ignore them? What about my goals, my projects, my grocery shopping, my waiting accountant? What about all that, Mr. Man of God?"

I was shocked, appalled, and disbelieving...

I read further to get more insight.

How to Prune the To-Do

David Allen's best-selling books, such as *Getting Things Done*, show us the way to do this without the uneasiness of wondering if we've neglected something important by pruning the tasks.

His premise is that all those niggling little projects we've ever thought of, regardless of how huge and inspiring, or small and pesky, are rattling around in our brains 24/7, using up valuable processing space, until we download all of them and record them somewhere.

Allen says it's perfectly OK to trundle tasks that don't pull their weight (i.e., really contribute to our heartfelt dreams and desires, and/or the significantly smoother functioning of daily life), right onto the "Future/Back Burner" section of our planners, without a whisper of guilt.

This is because if we had ten lifetimes all at once we wouldn't be able to get done everything we want to—that's just how the mind/ego works. Our brains go so much faster and farther than our bodies, if we let our brains run the show, we'll burn out early and often.

The point is to get them all down where they won't get away, and/or take up mind space every moment.

Asking ourselves some version of the question "Does this contribute to...?" for each item on at least today's to-do list helps us figure out when getting a massage trumps going over last quarter's sales figures one more time. Asking ourselves questions like this can help us recognize that taking a few minutes to respond to a child's playful overtures is just as important as never looking up from the computer.

The Back Burner section of the endless task list is how the Reverend could trim three-quarters of his list without a care in the world. Or if his mind, or yours, doesn't really sweat that stuff too much, scissors work just fine, too.

Sometimes it helps to reframe how you look at the items on your list. I love that in her book, *Lists that Saved My Life,* marketing expert Angel Tuccy keeps referring to "things I want to accomplish" instead of "things I have to get done." Doesn't it sound so much more expansive and purposeful, rather than harried? This gives us another way to look at individual items and decide if they really reflect how we want to do our lives, or if it's better to delete them.

The Case for Little Pieces of Paper

They really do get a bad rap, don't they? Scarcely a time management system refrains from dishing on those little pieces of paper we scribble phone numbers, appointments, directions, and notes on, only to lose them in the shuffle. It's usually when we don't have our official calendar or cell phone for taking down the notes in a hurry that we reach for them.

Count me a rebel on this topic because I think the bits of paper are brilliant! How else are we going to record those flashes of inspiration that shimmer through our minds at the speed of light? By the time we find our organizer or the right place on the phone to record it, or much, much worse, assure ourselves we will remember such a dazzling brainstorm, it's long gone.

Why take the chance? Those breakthroughs usually come from your intuition, attempting to help you get something accomplished at just the perfect time or finding the answer to a problem you've been working on. The first step is to make sure you've got plenty of those little blank pieces of paper (or sticky notes, 3x5 cards, or whatever) nearby so you can grab one in nanoseconds to write the info/idea down. Second, you need a central place where you can add them to the appropriate list to act on them at the right time.

I attach mine with an appealing paper clip to a nearby page of my paper calendar and go through them once or a few times a day if the ideas are rolling in fast. Whatever doesn't really need doing in the next couple days goes onto one of my informal running task lists, such as "shopping," "work stuff," "blog ideas," or the calendar.

What's on for today I prioritize—most important one on top and others below as time or convenience allows. When I'm finished, I give them a star or smiley face and toss them in a cool box, so I can see the "Dones" pile up. If I've been getting in a little rut of procrastination, I give myself the little note and a star for even the dumbest, smallest tasks to get me going on a roll again.

As always, what works is what works best for you, not some rigid system designed by someone who might be a stranger unto you!

Intuition Hack

Here's a counterintuitive thought. From one guru I heard, "The longer the to-do list for today, the longer you should meditate." So, I'm not there yet. However, the ten-minute *Sit Quietly, Do Nothing* meditation has been very valuable when my brain is fiercely bubbling with thoughts of all I "must" achieve today. The extra few minutes it takes pays off hugely in calming down my harried brain.

Your intuition gets a chance to kick in, and any of these things can occur to you:

- A quicker way to dovetail the tasks.
- Realizing the most important one or two tasks, if completed, might make several others unimportant for now.
- As the wildly reckless minister would suggest, drop some tasks completely.
- The short respite might also help you shift your outlook to see the big list as a fun challenge to do.
- Ways to make most or all the tasks more humorous.

Wow! Maybe more than 10 minutes is worth it.

Goals – To Declutter or Not to Declutter?

In the spirit of first decluttering the guilts, goals, or as some of us like to call them, "dreams," is one key place where "you do you" is vital. How you tackle them does not have to be exactly as some expert tells you to do it. Your dreams or goals don't have to match anyone else's, and they are very unlikely to do that anyway.

Goals are simply a bright reflection of the unique person you are, what resonates with your soul. They can be used to focus on whatever you'd like to declutter in your life. **And they're a wonderful place to put some of that energy freed up by all the decluttering efforts you've already put time into!**

Everyone has goals, whether they write them down or not, or whether they call them that or not. Even a person who seems to float through life focused on loving others, but without a lot of well-defined projects on the agenda, may be living out their goals or dreams.

If, however, you feel a strong pull towards accomplishing visible results that you can check the box on, making a big list of what calls out to you is a fun way to start. As with any brainstorming, it's good to initially make the list as fast as you can without editing as you go, or you will discourage and limit yourself. You can add to it if you think of other things in the next few days.

When you think you've written down all you can come up with for a while, you can look over them again, and see which ones you want to work on in the next year or so, and which could go on the back burner for a while. Some you will see are more along the line of "fairy godmother goals," that is, you probably won't spend a lot of time on them as they seem so far out of your current realm, but if they fell into your lap, you would happily receive them!

Decluttering Your Goals

Some of the items on your list are really other people's dreams, or their goals for you, which you don't have to take on or agree with. These are ripe for decluttering. But how do you declutter your goals? Take this list as well as any others you can find from the past and go through them with an eagle eye. Ditch any that are clearly outdated and don't interest you anymore. As I mentioned a few pages ago, we aspire to several more lifetimes of projects that we have time for, so don't feel bad about saying 'bye' to the duds. Carry forward ones that still seem relevant.

Add in ones that you dreamed about in your tender youth and have long since given up on. Throw in the wild ones, even if you think there's no way on God's green earth. For example: When it comes to cars, I am about as bored as a person can be. If it drives, gets good mileage, and doesn't hassle me with problems, I'm good with it. I used to have a '99 Honda Accord with 274,000 miles on it, and I was about to up my mental cutoff point on that baby from 300,000 miles to 500,000, figuring, "Why not? It's paid for," when someone offered me a deal I couldn't refuse on a new one.

One day I was driving down I-25 in Denver, and I saw the most amazing black sports car, with a rear spoiler (I think that's what it's called) so tall it almost hid the top of the car. I didn't even know what brand it was. I yelled at my female passenger to take a picture, which I showed my son. He said, "That's a freakin' Lamborghini!" So, okay, I want one. It's on my list now (fairy godmother goal).

Life coach Michael Neill, author of *Supercoach, 10 Secrets to Transform Anyone's Life*, says it's good to hang on to that fairy godmother list, as it's amazing how many of them just show up out of nowhere. Case in point. I just laugh when I think about my Lamborghini, but darned if it didn't appear in a multi-level marketing catalog I just saw, as one of the grand prizes for reaching "X" level in the company. And it was even a product I could bear to represent, so, you know, there's at least one way it could happen!

Look for Patterns in Your Goals

Elaine St James, author of *Simplify Your Life* and among the first to start the whole downsize movement, realized that her former list of 20 skills and goals she'd like to learn or accomplish, such as hang-gliding, Spanish, drawing, painting, gourmet cooking, studying the conflicts in the Middle East, mountain hiking, and joining a choral group was going to wear her out long before she left this earth.

When she looked at those things she really, truly enjoyed, she narrowed it down to five favorite activities, such as spending time with her husband, and quiet time in preparation for and doing her writing. They all had to do with writing or hanging out with family and friends. She put everything else on the back burner, with no further guilt, and a sigh of relief, and went on to write several best-selling books.

I had a big time in my twenties following one goal-setting guru's suggestion to write out 100 goals for my lifetime. The list went underground for several years and when I unearthed it, I was amazed to see how many I had already done, in one form or another.

Like St. James, I've narrowed down my scope in recent years, in the interest of not spreading myself so thin. My profession has been in land development as a civil engineer. In my youth, I had hoped to branch into transportation—well, work for the railroad, as it happens, my favorite form of transport. (Yes, haha, I know "train engineer," very funny.) But that's been scratched off the list. It just takes too long to learn the new expertise, plus I've already *so* done the engineering thing—It's time to move on!

Not too surprisingly, that list of 100 had some patterns, in keeping with my deepest interests (i.e., the ones that always give me a thrill of anticipation).

Now the groups are:

- Decluttering & organizing (doing, teaching, and writing about them).
- Making videos.
- Writing (I've had three books published, and two self-published).
- Creating colorful items of various kinds.
- Staying in shape and eating well.
- Have fun with family and friends.
- Planning my dream home, which will be solar-powered and otherwise self-sustaining.

This is substantially smaller than my previous *load* (Is it significant my mind chose *load*?). My two sons are grown, fantastic, and self-supporting, so that simplifies things a lot.

The main thing I've learned from my life of following many passions is that as compelling as they often are, I've gotten by far the most satisfaction out of having fun with my troops. Sometimes we've been working on a project together, sometimes we've been growing up together (like my kids, ex-husband, and I), and sometimes we're doing nothing much of note.

But without friends or family as an integral part of my life (and I'm probably more goal-oriented than average), the successfully completed projects don't mean a heck of a lot to me in the long run.

The point of goals is that they cause you to grow as a person in order to achieve them, more than whatever the individual goals are. And that growth comes from the process, not simply the endpoint. Elaine St. James' list of favorite activities are all ongoing ones, rather than specific projects. Paring down to just what she enjoyed led to her outstanding financial success. She didn't start out with a certain dollar figure in mind.

S.M.A.R.T. Goals Can Be Stupid

Denver law-of-attraction expert Jonathan Manske, author of *The Law of Attraction Made Simple: Magnetize your Heartfelt Desires*, says, "S.M.A.R.T goals can be stupid." Just because it's Specific, Measurable, Achievable, Relevant, and Timely doesn't mean it will lead to a feeling of fulfillment when achieved. Many times, we set some random goal that seems to be appropriate to our skills and interests, or is inspired by an outside force, such as friends and family, or TV advertising.

Maybe we have a go at it, but wonder why we feel empty when we accumulate the target dollar amount in the bank, big expensive toy, or a fancy wardrobe without thinking about what our real dreams are, and how that goal fits in.

Manske advises that you start by identifying the feeling you are working towards, and then developing S.M.A.R.T. goals out of that. These feelings don't easily fit into the "check off the box" focus of many goal-setting schemes. Rather than a lifestyle, these feelings may be more like a way of being, such as: being of service; being curious; and being a life-long learner.

Fulfillment, meaning, and purpose all come from goals such as these, however you carry them out with your projects and deliberate habits.

"A good way to find out if you're starting at this upper level," Manske says, "is to imagine yourself a ghost floating around at your own funeral, listening to what people are saying about you."

"If they say, 'Oh, yeah, Jonathan doubled his income!' that ghost is going to hate that that's their big memory of him."

"But if they say something like, 'Wow! He really made a difference in my life. He really helped me out.' Then that ghost is going to feel much happier!"

This exercise is designed to take the focus off of what's cluttering our lives and onto what we'd like our lives to be. Then it's easier to develop a compelling reason to reorganize and possibly jettison some of the clutter. We can keep our sights on what's truly important, being and doing who we really are.

This may seem a little self-absorbed, but it isn't, really. I believe we all have beneficial talents that we were born to express, in aid of our fellow humans, and in gratitude for the life God's given us. Your dreams and goals are huge indicators of your special talents, so working toward them is important, not just for you, but for the world. By the same token, squandering our energy on a lot of unneeded stuff is a waste of our lives and passions.

First Declutter the Guilts

That again? Hey, it has to be said. If you're the one who protests, "What if I love my S.M.A.R.T. goals, my checklists, my spreadsheets, etc.?" You do you! We need you in this world as well!

Being more on the "visualize and feel good about your goals" side of the spectrum, I was recently cracked up to learn that according to more than one study[10], thinking ahead about potential obstacles between you and your goals increases the likelihood substantially of them being achieved.

Also, look around at your life with extra creativity to see if some of the old goals have arrived without your noticing. For 25 years I kept saying I wanted an office on the south side of the house on the 2nd floor overlooking a beautiful garden. A few months ago, I thought "Hang on! Say, hasn't my office, for the past 3 years, been on the south side of my house? Sure, it's only on the mezzanine level instead of the 2nd floor, but still! And there's the back garden down there! Sure, it needs some substantial work to be what you'd call beautiful, but still! Dang! I'm already mostly there!" The only thing missing was a live-in cook to bring me my meals and high tea on a tray with a rose, but who knows?

---

[10] Gollwittzer, P., & Oettingen, G. (2011). Planning Promotes Goal Striving. In Handbook of Self-Regulation: Research, Theory and Applications (pp. 162–180). New York, NY: The Guildford Press.

PART III
CLEAR THE POSSESSIONAL CLUTTER – YOUR BELONGINGS, YOUR 'STUFF'

Seeing the Forest *and* the Trees

I picked up a magazine article from a famous women's magazine I'd been saving for a couple years (!) to read. It showcased photos and a few words of organizing wisdom from several of the magazine's department heads. I'm always combing these articles with razor intensity for any unique organizing tips I hadn't heard of before to make sure I haven't left out anything important in my writing about organizing.

Phew! Most of them I had already heard before—things like "Start with the least emotional items first and work your way up," and "Have big boxes handy for 'put back,' 'donate,' 'sell,' 'trash',," and "Think about whether it's worth the space it's taking to store it." Yes, yes, all good, all tried and true. I felt safe I hadn't missed anything important, except that I had.

Eventually it dawned on me: the bigger impact was the forest, not the trees. All these people live in New York City, the land of the mega-expensive real estate. And not being multi-gazillionaires, they all dealt with modestly-sized apartment homes.

Two photos in particular hit me hard: In one, the lifestyles editor was displaying her charmingly organized clothes closet, which was about one-third the size of my walk-in closet out here on the prairie. Yeah, I already sort clothes by type. And, in rainbow-color order. Got that. But what chilled me to the marrow was the thought, "Are those all the clothes she has?"

Then there was the home office of the cooking editor. A teeny-tiny kitchen desk with requisite wall calendar above it, tiny laptop/netbook thingy for planning meals, paying bills, etc., and two 5" x 8" ring binder notebooks sitting neatly off to the side. One was for takeout menus, and one for recipes — "so dinner's handled," was how she put it. "That's all *she* has?" I yelled in my head, shocked.

With foreboding I went and inspected my relatively modest collection of cookbooks and wondered when I last used any of them. Two years? Granted, I'd been doggedly busy those two years just making a living, but still! Then I looked at them with the purging eye to see which I could get rid of.

Not my grandmother's cookbook with her hand-written notes, and amazing recipes for things like Prize Gruel and Braised Possum! Not my Martha Stewart *Quickcook* book! Not the two church cookbooks featuring my late mother's recipes in print! Not the *Cooking for Two* cute little romantic mini-dinners in splendid 1970's photos! Hopeless!

Time out. Let's take a break from this mini-drama and refer to the first rule of decluttering (See the Mind Clutter chapter.) which is:

First, Declutter the Guilts

The New Yorkers may have traded storage space to live in the city of their dreams; the rest of us may have more room to spread out (and still be living in the home of our dreams). Neither situation is inherently wrong in any way; it's about what works for you.

I know that now, but when I started my organizing company, I was a little worried. I lived in a larger house then and I wondered if I'd fallen prey to the common tendency to expand my worldly goods to fill it up. I didn't want to be a hypocrite, for sure! So, I hired a seasoned professional organizer to check it out. She said, "Wow, you don't have much stuff!" What a relief!

That said, the guidelines of feng shui still gave me an opportunity to increase my frisky energy by releasing that which I didn't really need. They apply whether I live in an itty-bitty home or have stacks of room.

(I could just as easily extract the handful of recipes my mom had contributed to the church cookbooks and donate the rest of the two books. I didn't really need more recipes for potato casserole and peanut butter bars any way. I could even bite the bullet and donate my grandmother's 1941 cookbook to a historical museum. I'd recently learned authors of historical fiction appreciate such sources for glimpses of everyday life. Two chances to feel better by letting go, and eight inches of bookshelf freed up.)

Obviously, I sort of care where the decluttered stuff goes to and hope it will be appreciated in its new home, but this is completely optional, especially when the time it takes to figure out how to re-home items becomes an excuse to not bother downsizing. Give yourself permission to donate or toss the stuff without a backward glance, especially if it's beyond its useful life.

The extra belongings we have no use for and don't even care about that much still impact us. They're hanging out in our subconscious saying, "Hi, remember me? The un-made decision, cluttering up your life! Draining away your calm and resolve!"

Owie!

Stagnant stuff drags us down to an almost unbelievable degree, which only becomes evident when it's cleared out.

By the way, the alleged "5-6 hours a week" mentioned earlier in Part I? You can gain that much time simply by decluttering and organizing your possessions! That doesn't even include the extra time you gain from decluttering your emotions and physical body.

Those 5-6 hours are basically the estimated 55 minutes a day that we Americans lose, looking for stuff we can't find. (!)

Sound crazy? Sound like way too much? Think about the time spent looking for keys, purse or wallet, favorite shirt, (suddenly) wildly important piece of paper. It could even be time spent stalling and procrastinating about getting the ladder out of the garage to switch out a smoke-detector battery. You can *see* it plain as day, but the thought of pulling out all the stuff that seems to have been stacked in front of it since the last time you used it eighteen months ago makes you think a bit, and put it off once again...

Hmm. Maybe 55 minutes a day doesn't cover it...

Being able to put your hands on what you need in less than a minute, or without moving more than one other item to get to it, is a great goal to set as you declutter and organize. Time spent searching endlessly for needed items is always frustrating, annoying, and downright debilitating, even when it comes in dribs and drabs, and it adds needless stress to your life.

Plus, let's face it. These days, time is the new money. People with jobs are often working longer hours to make up for staff shortages or laid-off colleagues, so spare time is at a higher premium than ever. The currently unemployed have time, but don't need the extra stress. They need to remain cheerful, and optimistic, which is much easier when spaces are shipshape and functioning smoothly.

Besides, our time *is* our life. Fritter it away and we've frittered away our lives, with little to show for it. I bet you could make some serious inroads into a long-term project with 55 spare minutes a day. Even if you did nothing more "useful" than stare into space (meditation) for those 55 minutes, I guarantee your life would be calmer, more focused, more fun, and more productive!

What Ties Us to Our Stuff So Tightly?

I've heard we're as attached to our possessions as we are to our children and, as women's self-defense expert Melissa Soalt stated, "The flip side of the maternal instinct is the killer instinct." (!) Sometimes we'll fight just as fiercely to protect our belongings as if our little darlings were threatened. What's up with that?

Here are some possibilities:

We view material things as a substitute for love. We may have even been "bought off" on occasion by a harried or mostly absent parent who couldn't spend enough time with us. So, we learned to value things more than interactions. We could count on our things to "be there" for us when our people weren't, and we got very upset when those things were lost or taken away.

If we buy into the cultural hype of "The one who dies with the most toys wins!" it becomes easy to identify our value with the value of our belongings. I, for example, am a green-and-white striped love seat with red accent stripes, a cheap framed poster of Audrey Hepburn in *Breakfast at Tiffany's,* my computer, my 6-year-old car, and a few items of clothing that make me feel super-cool when I wear them. Get the idea? Hmm. Am I giving myself away? I really do have self-confidence. Honest!

After World War II, the powers-that-be decided to promote consumerism and planned obsolescence as a way of stimulating the economy. They succeeded so well it's now considered practically the Prime Rule of Consumerism: any appliance, vehicle, or electronic item should be replaced after __ years (fill in the blank with a low, one-digit number), as it's not nearly as good as the latest version of the item—even if the old one still works fine.

On top of that we still have remnants of the 1930's Depression-era frugality. With some justification people felt the need to hold on to absolutely everything with any serviceable life left in it, for fear that one would never be able to afford to buy it again. Ever!

The pain of letting go of an item, even one that's a whole lot of nothing special, is not as inexplicable as it turns out, after all. Brain research shows the parts of our brain[11] that light up when we struggle to part with a belonging are in the same areas that indicate a minor pain, such as a paper cut, or a mild burn[12]. Many canny retailers have taken advantage of this by making it super easy to handle and try out their products in the store. Basically, once we've already held the item in our hot little hands, it becomes ours, and we *must* have it.

Sometimes we pretend we truly needed some high-priced gadget we bought because we're embarrassed by how much it cost.

And there are the dozens, if not hundreds, of mementos, valuable antiques, and just plain junk, tightly held on to, from the fear we'll forget the beloved ancestors they remind us of if we let go of the items.

All these scenarios basically boil down to one emotion—fear. Fear of loss, fear of abandonment, fear of looking silly, fear of change. Fear, or pain, is not always easy to change since we can

---

[11] An SK et al. (2009).To discard or not to discard: the neural basis of hoarding symptoms in obsessive-compulsive disorder. Mol Psychiatry. 2009 Mar;14(3):318-31. doi: 10.1038/sj.mp.4002129. Epub 2008 Jan 8. PMID: 18180763.

[12] Tolin DF et al. (2012). Neural mechanisms of decision making in hoarding disorder. Archives of General Psychiatry, 69, 832-841.

get used to it. As one of my wise clients commented, "Clutter is like pain. We get used to it, and just keep putting up with it."

There are numerous ways to "conquer" fear, some of which are really just a matter of becoming aware of it. Who knew, for example, that one could simply take a photo of late Aunt Jess's valuable Ming vase, which doesn't even remotely match our decorating style, and then sell the sucker, ASAP?

Put the photo in a pretty little album filled with pictures of Aunt Jess, along with some of her letters, and you have a fitting tribute to that delightful woman. You were never going to forget her anyway. After all, she's the one who called you "doll baby" till you were in your twenties, took you on a balloon ride, and went with you to the mall to get her ears pierced for the first time at age 82, right along with you!

If you still feel an urge to honor the beloved person's memory, donate the money received from selling the valuable item to that person's favorite charity, or use it as a one-time gift to help out a friend or family member, as she or he might have done.

Embarrassed about spending a fortune on that massage bed gathering dust in the guest room, or the spectacular mountain bike ditto in the garage, that you shuffle past shamefacedly daily? Solution: Sell it, so it doesn't keep reminding you of your uncomfortable spending decisions.

The point is: we don't live in a vacuum. We're all products of our environment, and there are some pervasive influences that may have led to our over-collection of stuff, not only the societal ones, but personal competition (keeping up with the Joneses) and simply the childlike joy of adding to our toys, receiving gifts, and going for the gold...and diamond, earrings.

Don't waste a lot of time beating yourself up about it. It may be fun to try to understand how you got that way, but don't stay there too long. By the time you figure it out, you could have had the hall closet *and* the garage sorted!

The tricky part, as with many projects in life, is not comprehending the "problem," but getting started on a solution. And just as the purchases and retention of stuff is largely emotional, that which finally gets you off dead center to declutter is emotional, too.

We're inspired by something that touches our heart *or* triggers our fight-or-flight! See which speaks to you in a clearer voice.

Where Do You Start and What's Your Motivation?

Of the three clutter agendas, imagining the possessional clutter handled makes the dream life easiest to visualize.

What is your dream for your space? Is it:

a. Model home beautiful, showing off your artwork and style instead of stacks of stuff?
b. Army barracks minimalist, with nothing holding you back from an action-packed life of adventure?
c. A cozy family abode with room for fun family activities?
d. A restful haven to recharge from your hectic life?
e. Just some noticeable improvement over the current chaos?

Or, for your office: what inspires you?

I imagine myself a tycoon with a desk as big as Kansas, and only the current piece of paper I'm working on visible. The rest is tucked neatly away or being handled by "my people." I'm smoking a fat cigar, of course (kidding), and doing some efficient wheeling and dealing. This image makes me laugh, but I do swoon at the sight of a large, uncluttered desk.

My favorite vision for my home is the well-stocked vacation condo: nicely decorated, bare necessities there, no clutter. It gives me a refreshing springboard for my vacation adventures, or a distraction–free spot to work on the Great American non-fiction book. It also helps my whole life feel a bit like a vacation, or at least the relaxed approach to it, even when I'm working hard and mixing it up with daily life!

Has it been so long you forgot how to hope for your ideal space? Don't worry, it will come back to you. Write down ten things you'd like to do in your ideal workday and leisure day. What would your home look like to support those days?

Imagine if your workspace or entire home were all as streamlined as your dreams would like them to be! What results would you get?

- Your roomie comes home with $1000 worth of spotless chrome he just bought for his motorcycle, and the living room has all the space and order needed to spread it out and get it organized (true story, believe it or not).

- You simply feel a sense of contentment knowing your family home is operating as smoothly as it can.

- It's Saturday, the house is in the order you'd like, and you and your troops are footloose and fancy-free to do whatever you like. What would you do? How would you spend that time?

- You can welcome visitors, even those that arrive with little notice--no need for an armed sentry.

- It's a joy to come home to your space and feel the time spent there nourish you instead of stress you.

This was the question I've asked audiences many times: "How would you spend that time freed up by being decluttered and organized?" Taken by surprise, they often can't think of anything more unusual than spending a lot more time reading. At first, I was mildly appalled, having envisioned things like "go ziplining," "learn jewelry design," and "volunteer at a children's hospital." Then I thought "Hey! Declutter your criticism!" Who am I to say what's exciting to people or not?

(Plus, sometimes it takes a minute to remember what your fondest dreams might have been, if you've gotten in the habit of back-burnering them.)

So, definitely dream your own dream, and use it as a jumping-off point to get more of whatever it is in your life.

My all-time favorite decluttering story came courtesy of Edna, a lovely 70-something I met at a networking event. She said she and her husband decided to sell their two-story, 3-bedroom suburban home and move to a 1400-square-foot townhouse. The sale went so fast they had to get out in two weeks.

She said, "We had lived there for 50 years, and we had to get rid of 70% of our stuff. The feeling was one of the best I've had in my life!"

This was a carrot disguised as a stick.

Which works better to inspire you, the carrot or the stick? Don't feel bad if you are likely to get in motion more readily to the stick. To some extent, it's human nature. Think about how much harder you'd work to get back $25,000 you had lost, as opposed how much effort you'd put into earning an extra $25K in the first place.

Here's an example:

Stick

An impending move? An involuntary downsizing of your home space? The threat of arriving company you can't bear to let see the house this way? A natural disaster? You and the kids going out of your freaking minds with all the junk everywhere?

Carrot

Perhaps you've decided to become a Quaker, or you aspire to match the tranquility of your home to that of your serene Japanese garden, or you realize you can't continue to exist until your home makes the cover of your favorite decorating magazine.

Let's face it. As with the $25K, if clutter is what's kicking your butt, chances are it's the two-by-four motivation that will finally get you to move a muscle!

My friend, Judy, had wanted to remodel and personalize her bedroom for more than two years. But it wasn't until a minor plumbing disaster resulted in water in the bedroom closet that she finally moved forward on that project.

Since everything had to come out of the closet to allow the workers in to do the repairs, she started from there and worked her way out.

Judy moved all the memorabilia and craft and sewing supplies out of her closet into another room to simplify the bedroom ambience and make it more soothing, added a canopy over her bed, and replaced carpet and linens.

She used the experience as a springboard to declutter her whole house because, as she said, "I realized I really just like the look of flat surfaces with nothing on them except photos of my kids and grandkids."

The stick turned into the carrot, and something far more glorious: a transformation and a vast improvement in her life.

Fear as a Motivator

Staying in a campground in bear country for the first time in decades, I found interesting additions to each campsite: cool metal bear-proof cupboards.

Nearly the size of a small dumpster, there's room inside for all your food, cooking gear, and even toiletries. Anything with a whisper of a hint of producing food-like odors is required to be stashed, except when directly in use, or it might be confiscated.

I was struck by how *organized* all the campsites looked. No dirty pots and pans stacked around, no falling-over bags of potato chips, no syrup dribbles on the ground. Clean as a whistle!

Now there's some fear-based motivation at work to inspire you to tidiness!

Fear is a fairly reliable motivator, even when the stakes are not quite as high. You may feel like you're going to die if the guests you've invited to dinner see what a wreck your house is, but it's just an illusion. You won't die from disorder nor embarrassment.

However, do feel free to use the thrill of flirting with death to spur you on to new heights of order and clutter-free-ness. Millions have used it before, and it has served them very well. You probably have that one terrifying person (friend, or more likely relative or in-law, spouse's ex, etc.) whose surprise arrival in ten minutes sends you into a tailspin of compressing time to unclutter the house at warp speed rather than have that person see it in its current state!

(BTW, it's no mistake that "Cleanliness is next to Godliness" is the 11th Commandment. It's there to keep you safe!)

Make It Fun, and It's More Likely to Get Done

As you've heard by now, this is an underlying theme for this book, and a big tip to transform all these intense declutter agendas into enjoyable adventures:

Make it fun!

Make it a game, a challenge, whatever you want. Even if you don't feel it right at the moment of impact ("Yes, they are actually arriving in ten"), switch as quickly as you can to fun mode.

When I was young, I used to play a game with my four younger cousins. When we were assigned kitchen cleanup after meals, I pretended to be a mean witch threatening dire consequences if the kitchen wasn't 100% shipshape when I got back in ten minutes. Then, I'd leave the room muttering skeptical words and tiptoe back in immediately, pretending to be a super-kind princess come to help them get to 100%. We'd scurry around, thrilled to be in danger, and operating at top efficiency!

You guessed it; after the ten, I'd leave again and return as the witch, ready to pounce, running my finger along the top of the fridge, and finding only cleanliness throughout! Well, good enough for make-believe, at least. Then I'd depart in fake fury that I'd been cheated out of my horrible fun.

A dumb game, for sure, but we never tired of it. For the most part, the stakes are really not a whole lot higher than that in our adult lives, but instead of getting a kick out of it and letting it kick us into gear, we spend the time flying around with dread roiling in our stomachs and a genuine feeling of stressed panic.

Not fun, but it could be. Up to you.

(Going out on a limb to guess that, just maybe, some of that abject terror has at least a few sprinkles of the kid's thrill of possibly getting in trouble? So maybe it's more fun than it sounds like.)

The Woman's Hero's Journey

One of my male friends was mildly indignant on my behalf when I told him how I wouldn't let an unexpected visitor enter my home, which was temporarily a shambles due to just having started not one but two whirlwind projects that required stuff spread on every available surface.

The visitor was one of my clients coming to pay an invoice, but I had forgotten he was supposed to stop by sometime soon. "He was even bringing me a big check!" I laughed, thinking my friend would *totally* understand, as would any of my women friends.

He did *not* understand, and went on a rant saying, "If somebody stops by without notice, it's on them if they find a mess! Why do women always think their house has to be perfect all the time no matter what?"

I was so taken aback by his tirade I almost missed that I and all of womanhood were being championed here!

Then I wandered off into one of my ponderings about just why that was and decided it might be an instinctive throwback to cave person days, when your life depended on the tribe accepting you. Perchance if it got around your housekeeping was slovenly, you'd be passed by in the mating game, or worse, cast out by the tribe to die.

OK, total speculation here. But there must be some (barely) rational reason that makes it feel like it's a life-and-death matter.

Time for a mental sign: "Showing up at my house unexpectedly is at your own risk. Deal with it!"

Stick:

1. See above ("They'll be here soon").

OR

2. Pretend your house is threatened by a natural disaster, and you have an hour to take out what you value most. What would go with you and what would be left behind? This is actually a very interesting exercise; it really clarifies what possessions you truly value the most. If there's a fire, you may only have seconds to grab something handy that you love, but an hour broadens the scope to be able to carry out the highest value possessions.

Carrot:

Show your courage! Leap into the fray and actually invite some people over for a get-together in the near future. That gives you a chance to do a more thorough job, and a lot more control over the situation. You could still have fun with it with checklists, milestones, rewards. Or simply stay relaxed and think about the joy you will bring to your guests, who are likely looking so forward to it, and may not even give a rat's patootie what your house looks like.

Inspired by Kindness

Are you wicked tender-hearted? This one's nearly foolproof for you:

Stick:

Simply think of how someone less fortunate could have been enjoying that unused item you've been unwilling to use or get rid of all these years.

Boom, you're there!

After all, if your friend's kid was just starting her or his first household, you wouldn't hesitate to ditch—I mean gift—your never-used lame utensils on her or him, would you?

Pretend all the people who'll be buying your stuff at the thrift store are your friend's kid instead of some faceless stranger. Or even remember your own younger self who would have been tickled to pay $5 for an essential $50 item.

Not much of a stick in this situation, just a tiny, tiny amount of guilt and the willingness to envision their joy!

Carrot:

Decluttering can give your social conscience a feel-good kickstart. When you pass along items that are moldering away in your house unused for years, to someone who can put them to use immediately, you get a green star!

Even if you sell the item rather than donate it, you are reviving resources that would otherwise go to waste. I've been reading about how much water it takes to manufacture various items that make our lives easier and *golly* it's an eye-opener, never mind the enlargement of our carbon footprint.

In the green hierarchy of goodness, reuse outclasses recycling, and they're both infinitely cooler than landfilling, but even landfilling is way better than keeping around a bunch of broken-down junk or flawless "new, with-tags" items that weigh you down.

Everyone wins!

ROI[13] as Motivation

Stick:
How much does your unused stuff cost you? Do you like numbers? Let's do the math.

Emotionally? Zero to infinity. Stress, bogged-down creativity, that helpless, out of control feeling...too many variables to calculate a dollar value.

Physically? Stubbed toes, conked heads, unrestful sleep...again, a wide range.

Real Estate-wise? Maybe you're not renting three storage spaces @$100/month (total cost/year $3600) like one woman I heard about, you just have it around the house that you're paying for anyway. But consider:

100 square feet used to store stuff you never use in an average 2200-square-foot house that costs, say, $1500/month, is confiscating about $818/year worth of your space. Not too bad,

---

[13] Which, I know you know, means "Return on Investment."

unless you keep it there for 10 years, or have, perchance, more than 100 square feet of unused stuff...

Carrot:

Think what you could do with that 100 sq. ft? (That's 10' x 10'.)
Dance?

Lay out your catfishing gear and get it organized for the next catfishing trip?

Leave room for the dog to chase its tail?

Have 20 relatives over for a rockin' holiday meal instead of just 6?

The possibilities are endless.

Here, both carrot and stick offer a lot of scope. It is rather "inspiring" to put fingers to calculator and figure out how many dollars are going to waste.

Plus, your money-making project wheels could be spinning with ideas for how to make bank on the freed-up space. Guitar lessons? Short-term rental? Music videos? Seminars on...something?

Not to mention the investment in your joy and peace of mind, and for the room to spread your wings out even farther!

Pressed for Time

Hang on. How's that going to work? How is spending those millions of hours[14] it'll take to organize this whole place going to magically free up time?

Stick:

How many minutes a day do we spend looking for missing-in-action keys, paperwork, tools, clothing, snacks we hid from other family members, even cars, occasionally, when we park in a big

---

[14] This is only an illusion. It takes less time than you think!

lot? It's not only when we can't remember where we last left the Phillips screwdriver, or the embroidery instructions, it's also the time spent worrying that we won't be able to find them. This may be 5x or 10x the time spent actually looking for them.

If you kept a log, you might find, as previously mentioned, that you're wasting upwards of an hour a day on all those dismal, depressing efforts. Ugh!

Carrot:

That 5, 6, 7 hours a week you could free up by decluttering and organizing? What could you do with that? In addition to the ideas mentioned above, including reading, you could:

Take improv lessons.

Hike up a 14-'er.[15]

Watch the whole Indie 500 without feeling guilty. (Just threw that one in for a joke. I know y'all who watch it consider it a patriotic duty. There's no feeling guilty here.)

Pull together that custom photo book you've been threatening to make for six months (years).

Go ahead and take the time to organize the cat-fishing gear in the space you are also freeing up.

Write 3 hours on the Great American Novel AND go to a movie.

Go to a museum, or, you know, a car show.

Continue your quest to find the best fish-and-chips in town.

Listen to your loved ones.

You could also spend the time each day meditating, whose benefits multiply the time spent doing it (see the Mind Clutter section), reading a fun book, or listening to what the angels have to tell you, all rich rewards!

---

[15] Colorado term for a mountain peak at least 14,000 in elevation. We have 58 of them, not to boast.

Saving Money

Decluttering saves money, too. Let's face it, there's a fortune tied up in the items we've acquired without following through and putting them to good use in our lives. Let's see, if I spent an average of $5 on 100 items I forgot I had, that's $500. The average American family may have upwards of 100,000 items in their home. I assume that means things like paper clips, too, but I haven't even made a cursory estimate/inventory. I'm sort of afraid to.

What if the number of unused items is more like 5000? Then we're talking about a serious chunk 'o change.

Stick:

How embarrassing! You discover you've actually bought three sets of Allen wrenches, or pairs of pink Angora mules, when you only need one! Don't feel like the Lone Ranger; everyone does it if they have space to store things and forget about them.

Carrot:

By decluttering and organizing, you'll no doubt turn up those things you forgot you had, thus saving you from having to purchase them again when you truly need that handy item (should that ever actually happen).

You may even find a few things you don't need any more that are worth selling.

One friend of mine girded up her loins (gathered her courage) and sold over 50 items on Craigslist, including a car and a bunch of furniture.

At the extreme end of this continuum, by decluttering a significant chunk of the 100,000 items, you might even be able to move into a smaller house (if that makes sense with your other life circumstances, of course).

Stress Reduction

Stick:

According to a UCLA study[16], disorganization, and especially clutter, causes an increase in the stress hormone, cortisol. This is the one that can lead to reduced energy levels, feeling chaotic, interrupted sleep, and even weight gain.

The effect of disorganization ranges from mild to completely debilitating, depending on the obliviousness of the inmates of an establishment. It takes its toll on relationships, productivity, and general happiness, as it's almost inevitable that the tolerance for clutter/disorganization will not be uniform among the troops.

The same study indicated the women in the families experienced the most increased cortisol. Most men, and even older children, were not nearly as impacted by it. There you have it: science backing up what moms have known forever!

However, if clutter paralyzes you, you have a right to stake your claim for tidiness, regardless of what UCLA says is normal!

Carrot:

Feel the rush, baby! This is where the rubber meets the road! Those yummy feel-good chemicals (endorphins) show up almost immediately after you start the decluttering process; you don't even have to exercise for thirty minutes for the endorphins to kick in (See the "Declutter Basics" chapter.)

It starts as a trickle, with maybe a lot of resistance to letting go of anything "possibly useful," but as soon as you release the first item, the momentum builds till at some point you are surfing the thrill and laughing at the cortisol. Whether anyone else in the family joins you, the high is still available.

---

[16] Saxbe DE, Repetti R. No place like home: home tours correlate with daily patterns of mood and cortisol. Pers Soc Psychol Bull. 2010 Jan;36(1):71-81. doi:10.1177/0146167209352864. PMID: 19934011.

Now you know they're not being obstinate, only behaving normally, in a University-of-Southern-California-predicted way, you can add to your own enjoyment in seeing if you can Tom Sawyer them into pitching in. OK, maybe that's a stretch, but a good way to inject more fun for yourself, over there all tossing junk and snickering!

Eventually, the endorphin rush turns into a sense of peaceful satisfaction, as you get through more and more of the backlog.

A peaceful mind is a great carrot, and a wonderful ally for both the easy times and the more difficult ones. The need for organization is particularly strong when times are challenging. We need all the help we can get, then, and the knowledge that we're semi-on top of things on the home front can offset some of the feelings of lack of control over outside events.

Plus, how much more fun will it be not to have to keep a shotgun at the door to bar drop-in visitors from seeing the devastation?

Productivity/Creativity as Motivation

Stick:

As a kid, I was mesmerized by a scene at the end of Dr. Seuss' *The Cat in the Hat*. In the scene, the Cat comes back with an amazing machine and cleans up the whole house, recently trashed by himself, Thing 1, and Thing 2, in the time it takes Mother to walk up the block. I *loved* that scene: the instant transformation back to order; the chance for the C in the H to redeem himself and save the day in a spectacular way, and the same element of danger many of us feel when faced with unexpected visitors, especially moms!

Similarly, Dr. Seuss' *How the Grinch Stole Christmas* also fascinated me, with its scenes of the Grinch stealing every blessed thing related to Christmas from all the Whos' houses.

Only the forlorn wires of strings of lights with the bulbs taken out remained. I adored this part of the story!

How did I come to have such a twisted, unnatural attitude?

Simple. It's pure self-defense.

Sometimes all I do is walk through a room and it starts to disintegrate. Stuff seems to magically fly off shelves and all over flat surfaces, multiplying like rabbits as it goes.

On the other hand, it's a challenge for me to function at any task of work when there's clutter in my field of vision (see the UCLA study mentioned above).

Sure, if the wolf is at the door, and the deadline's right behind her, I channel the necessary tunnel vision to get that project finished. But, if I'm working on anything proactive and/or creative, clutter can be paralyzing. It invites procrastination and leaves me, as one of my poetic friends says, "nailed to the deck."

This is the opposite of the rush.

In desperation, I keep decorative objects to a minimum, so I can at least keep up with the Taking Care of Business items and the other boring necessities of life.

This bareness was so extreme that when my kids were growing up, my twelve-year-old son, a guys' guy if there ever was one, once complained about the lack of décor. "Shouldn't we have, like, more paintings or knickknacks or something?"

I'm no minimalist, as my visitors would agree, but I do adore a bit of restraint. Not sure if I was born that way or if my unusual (with respect to things) childhood was the cause, but it likely played a part.

Ask yourself what your childhood reveals about how you feel about the belongings/clutter/clear space paradigm. We each have different reactions to whatever went on in our youth with respect to that. Some of us will reproduce the stuff level of our parents' home; some will deliberately do the opposite. And it doesn't even necessarily matter whether we grew up happy in that home. It's a combo of that history, plus our own unique personality.

Don't be surprised if your attitudes and habits about your belongings have contradictions and mix-ups in their logic or illogic. (Declutter the guilts.)

Carrot:

The main thing, as expressed in the Mind Clutter section, is not to let that past take up too much time in the present, but to forge your own policy that allows you to create that which you came to create and build an environment which supports that. It's one of the most powerful motivators because it pairs a positive outcome with your own unique dreams.

Be a Rebel!

You're not going to be a pawn for those Madison Avenue hucksters!

You don't care if you don't have the latest version! The five-year-old one is good enough for you!

You don't buy the lie that it's our patriotic duty to consume!

You don't care if every surface in your home doesn't gleam with clean!

You don't care about those freaking hot-dog cookers, in-home weather stations, and six colors of blusher!

You're not going to let them send your clutter quotient and credit card balances sky-high!

It's all their fault!!

Declutter and organize! You'll get down to your classic value pieces in every department of your home, then you'll show those Philistines!

So, believe it or not, the rebel view actually represents a lot of what motivates me in decluttering, and in many areas of my life, despite my pathetic excuse for incendiary rhetoric. Rebel maybe not the best word for me, at least not as a convincing leader of the revolution. "Fierce, but quiet, non-conformist" is a more accurate term.

If you really want to amp up the rebelliousness, exact the perfect revenge. Learn how fun it can be to spend time rather than money with friends and family. Hard core!

Side note: The mess-maker rebellious? In organizer circles, it's been whispered that messy people are sometimes actually perfectionists. The story is, they secretly realize that the level of orderliness they truly crave is almost impossible to maintain, so they give up in hopelessness without even trying.

You Completely Adore It!

This may sound strange: One Christmas morning, with my traditional Christmas dinner and present opening to look forward to at a relative's house[17] at noon, I took the free morning and gave myself the gift of allowing myself to organize my pantry! Felt too swamped with work the rest of the year to justify taking that time for this yummy treat. How's that for festive?

Ok, I know there are those who would find this activity A LOT less fun than watching a NASCAR race, shopping for new clothes, going to a movie, or even cleaning the bathtub…And that is why some of us are professional organizers (mysteriously eccentric humans) and some of us, in sharp contrast, are not.

---

[17] A little bonus life tip: Always make sure you have relatives or friends who love to host the holidays, then you don't have to! See how that works? Be nice to them, offer to bring some wine, offer to clean up (it takes way less time and brain power than cooking the meal), and you will be sure to get invited back year after year. Problem solved!

Have Fun with It – Lush Budget Imagination

Remember that earlier exercise of imagining your house was about to be hit by a natural disaster, and you had an hour to decide what to take with you?

Well, this is the opposite. Instead, imagine you won the lottery, and for some strange reason, had to stay in your same house. Would you keep everything you had now, knowing you could easily afford whatever random item you might need in the future?

BTW, this is a good exercise for life in general. Unless we are quite unusual, we spend thousands of hours of our lives worrying about what could go wrong, even though most of these things never happen. (See the "Mind Clutter" chapter.)

Don't you think a case could be made for spending an equal amount of time imagining what could go right? It's just as likely as the opposite, and, in fact, **in many of our lives, wonderful things/miracles happen almost every day; thus, things going "right" is actually more likely!**

Bonus Motivation – Organizing is Biblical

I bet that comes as a surprise. Think about it. How can you "consider the lilies of the field," and subsequently "not worry about tomorrow, for tomorrow will worry about itself" (Matt. 6:34) if you have 13,276 unused items in your house that you're saving just in case you might need them someday?

And check out Eccl. 3:1 and 6: "There is a time for everything...a time to keep and a time to throw away." Also, does "divine order" mean order is divine?

I mentioned these passages at an Optimist's Club I spoke at, and one clever soul piped up with "Yeah, but it also says, 'Jesus saves!'"

And the Real You Shines Through

This book could also have been titled, *Clear the Space, Make Room for Yourself.*

You can do that in two ways. On the surface level, of course, when you declutter, put stuff away in a more organized manner, you're going to make room for yourself. Room on the kitchen counter, the dining table, the floor, the library shelves, the basement, the garage, etc.

You free up some solid real estate to expand your horizons into.

But the bigger opportunity comes when we realize clutter creeps up gradually over time, covering your surfaces, your decor, and your psyche like a thick layer of dust. It blurs the lines of all that personality you have hiding beneath it.

Here's the true payoff. All that heartwarming stuff I said back in the Declutter Basics chapter is what it's all about. When you declutter and organize, you not only liberate space, but you begin to see your own style again.

When you clear out the clutter and clear the space, you free up your soul to express its dazzling unique design in ideas, quirks, and problem-solving panache! Declutter the non-you!

Make room for yourself.

Streamline your life and open it up to amazing new possibilities!

Here's the Rush – How to Make Organizing and Decluttering Fun

Which to do first, declutter or organize? Decluttering is the hardest part of organizing for most people, as we must then make the decisions we've already been putting off. Don't make it harder by beating yourself up about your indecisiveness. Just keep telling yourself, "I've been busy!"

Remember this reassuring fact: All organizing projects basically boil down to three steps:

Sort, purge, organize what's left.

OR

Purge, sort, and organize what's left.

If you're good at making quick decisions, purge first. If not, sort first, to see how many of each item you really have. This makes it a little easier to let go of your thirteenth through twenty-second white shirts (unless, of course, that's what you wear every day).

Also, the clutter really is finite, regardless of how big the mountain seems. It just looks impossible because you're already stuck in all that stagnant energy.

For some, however, sorting first makes sense. Gather all the like items from around the house or office, then you can see what needs to be decluttered. You are less likely to willy-nilly throw something out that turns out to be your favorite, or the last one you had in the house of an often-used item, thinking you have another one in the basement. (Possible, though not likely.)

Anyway, the decluttering process has always fascinated me more, since it means we need to dig deeper into ourselves and work through the often-painful process of letting go. I figure the more we declutter, the less we have to organize.

Vow to go easy on yourself as you go through this process. Don't bother asking yourself why you haven't already gotten it done! We've all put in hard time on useless, debilitating activities, but even if every single project or hobby we took on was wholesome, productive, and Mom-approved, we'd still tackle way too many pursuits. It's the way humans are wired--especially in America, the land of the over-achieving goal-driven.

Where are you now? Take a clipboard and a legal pad, if you like to feel super-efficient, and walk around your whole home, writing down which areas get on your nerves with clutter or lack of organization. Take "Before" photos. You could do it with an electronic note taker on your phone, if you really want to feel wedding-planner efficient.

Where to Start?

The idea is to tackle the worst first. From your notes, identify the area of the house that bugs you the most. Starting with that one gives the quickest positive impact on your daily life. (Like my mom always said, "Make up the bed—the biggest item in the bedroom—and you'll be ready to attack the day!")

Still not sure where to start? Consider:

a. The "basement," or other long-term storage space. Then there's room to put the things you've decided to keep. There's something satisfying about rooting out the oldest of the old detritus, knowing you are not simply skimming the surface. However, this may seem an insurmountable obstacle, depending on what's in your basement. A less intimidating project is simply to carve some space out of that location to at least get you going.

b. Entrances, to avoid stressing out visitors or family as long as possible.

c. Kitchen, or home office—wherever you spend the most time.

d. Bedroom, to first create a restful haven to retreat to.

e. The point is, just start somewhere!

Schedule the time to declutter and organize. Think you can't possibly do that as you are just WAY too busy doing life? Well, let's face it. You have all that extra stuff now because you didn't take the time before to make the hard decisions. If someone offered you $500/hour to organize, I'll bet you'd find time to squeeze it in. Keep remembering those 5-6 hours a week. Eventually you'll break even.

When a little extra time opens up, whittle away at the snag that is always bugging you. Put away a few items. This may work better for you than blocking off a big chunk of time, as it may feel less daunting. Ask yourself, "What's one small thing I can do daily to shift it?" The relief from handling the worst area will make the rest of your list easier to deal with.

Get some help from a friend: Pair up and help each other with your decluttering projects, or just pick a day to both work on a hard project individually and call each other once an hour to make sure you're staying on track. It will feel less like a lonely toil.

Get some help from a professional: If you wouldn't dream of inflicting your mess on your friends, hire a professional organizer. They may know some shortcuts that would make the process so much quicker and less painful. Sometimes it just helps to have someone kind to talk over your memories of your stuff with; it helps you let go of the stuff. If they are wise, they will be non-judgmental; they will encourage you to continue letting go of the non-essentials and help you not to lose heart, nor give up.

The cost is reasonable, and the motivation of having an appointment with someone and paying them money has a galvanizing effect on the process. It gets done.

Where to Send Your Stuff

Sell expensive items you don't cherish any more through free classifieds, social media marketplaces, and consignment shops. This is where a professional organizer can help, too. They often have a line on extensive additional resources for getting your stuff sold at a better price. Warning, though: if what you want to sell is delicate china, "valuable" antiques, or other items of the original and super-expensive variety, don't be disappointed if you get much less for it than you think it's worth.

Many people of all ages, but especially the young, are now avoiding fussy, high-maintenance items that would have been treasured even a generation ago. You may have to settle for passing them on to someone who appreciates them at all, rather than holding out for the best price.

You could always have a garage sale, but don't do it on my account, unless you have an ocean of stuff to sell and garage sale season is either in full swing, or just a month or two away. Those things sitting in your house waiting for months is not what we're looking for here. Neighborhood associations often have an annual garage sale, which is a good time to tag along, so people have several places to shop in a small area. It can be fun to meet neighbors that way and see how your wheeler-dealer instincts play out. You might surprise yourself.

Estate sales are common, too, when you have a lot of nicer stuff to sell. These can even happen when no one has died and you simply want to get rid of a household of things. They are often handled by a professional, who will do some effective advertising for you. They'll also take a commission of at least 35%. Estate sales often happen inside the house, which gives more room to display your treasures, and will likely produce better prices for your items.

There are also companies that specialize in taking away large quantities of items for a fee,[18] and the best ones will sell, donate, or recycle as much as they can, which is part of their profit. This is a good solution if you don't care whether you make money on your stuff—you simply want it gone. The advantage over donating all to a charity is that some charities have restrictions

---

[18] The base fee for one Colorado company that does this is $150. The price goes up depending on the amount of stuff to move out.

on what they will take. On the other hand, many charities have gotten into the online business of selling their donated items, too, so more of it may find a loving home than it might have in the past.

In some instances, a tax deduction for charitable donations may exceed what you can get by selling items. Just be sure to list broad categories and approximate second-hand value of everything you donate. Take a few photos if the pile is large.

Decluttering Basics

Move everything out of the space you are decluttering. Whether a whole room, or just a single drawer or closet, remove all the items. Even if you end up putting many of the items back, as they are frequently used or well-loved, you will still have released that stuck energy. By considering each object, you put your mind at ease about the things you're keeping.

If you can, put kept items back in a slightly different place. Just this small step will refresh the space as well.

If one of the reasons in the motivation section of this chapter doesn't resonate with you, just keep asking yourself whether each item supports or takes away from the vision for your space or your time you came up with earlier.

Make it one of your goals to clear off all flat surfaces. Kitchen counters were meant for preparing tasty meals, not storing every scrap of paper that enters your home. Dining tables are for congenial meals, not ten years' worth of tax records and catalogs.

The floor is the ultimate flat surface, and feng shui is quite firm about keeping the floor clear of stagnant storage, to maximize your flowing energy (see below). Think: dancing, kids and pets running around, a temporary space to store the 600 boxes of Girl Scout cookies your daughter sold, whatever!

If you're the logical type, you probably realized you can't put 15 inches of books into a 12-inch-wide shelf. Group the books in fives and pick out your least favorite 1 or 2 from that group to get rid of. With less pain, you can weed out your lower-status-treasures, and methodically reduce the load. **When you look at the favorites, then the less beloved, it becomes much easier to see what's valuable to you and what can be weeded out.**

Always leave time at the end of the decluttering session to move the items to their next destination—misplaced items to their correct homes, trash bags to the curb, donations in the car to be dropped off at your earliest convenience, etc. Otherwise, your feeling of accomplishment will fizzle out once you lift your head from your decluttering frenzy.

Too late? Already drooping? Take a water and snack break, move completely away from the area, and read a book for twenty minutes or chat with someone. Get your mind right off the subject. After a bit you can re-focus on that "pared-down condo" vision, or whatever floats your boat, then go back in and tackle the distribution.

Feng Shui Basics

Feng shui dovetails beautifully with decluttering, because *every* feng shui treatise recommends starting by uncluttering your spaces. Feng shui philosophy states we are always interacting with the objects around us. (Quantum physics says roughly the same thing, oddly enough.)

Too many belongings, possessional clutter, meets us wherever we turn and slows us down faster than molasses in the crankcase. It saps our strength and robs us of our *joie de vivre*. Feng shui is spot on when it tells us clutter dissipates the lively energy in our homes and psyches.

This explains why we almost always feel dragged down when we enter a cluttered space. Those objects that have become forgotten, thus essentially useless, are latching onto you in an attempt to gain some of your energy for themselves. Did I really say that? No, I couldn't have, but there is something weird about how we lose our zest when we are around cluttered, stagnant stuff.

Observe your reaction next time you're in a messy place, and then, how much more energized you feel in a calm, uncluttered area. Even if you don't get any farther than "uncluttered" in your feng shui attempts, you'll have handled the biggest issue.

Feng shui defines clutter as "things we neither use nor love." Anything that is not cherished, or regularly put to use goes in the clutter category. Best for you if it's "sent to its next home."

The modern American feng shui version of that motto is, "Love it or use it; otherwise lose it!"

Organizing Basics

Before you get carried away with decluttering everything that isn't nailed down, ask yourself if you are a person whose main desire for their stuff is to create order, or one who loves displaying things—photos, *objets d'art*, books, and other items that define our place in the world.

Humans are naturally drawn to either order or display in what's pleasing to look at. These qualities can be combined, such as a when uniform set of dishes is stored in a glass-fronted cabinet, or a boatload of schedule notes, phone numbers, artwork, cartoons, are all jam-packed, and thus tidily confined, to a family bulletin board.

Display might be the fascinating arrangement of leather reins and bits dangling from matter-of-fact hooks near the front door of the active horse lover's home. Or it could be a small collection of shells commemorating all your trips to the ocean. It could be your own embroidered tea towels perking up the kitchen. A huge brandy snifter can hold dozens of matchbooks from the restaurants you've eaten at, with all the money you saved from not buying stuff you don't need!

I have a decorating book that showcases homes with wildly diverse interior design styles, ranging from the severest minimalism to the nearly Victorian in décor-crowdedness. I often show it to clients, asking them to identify what level display they are comfortable with. You should assess this for yourself in some way, so you are not bowing to pressure from someone else's comfort level of austerity.

Clutter is not the same as display, and you're not "wrong" if you love a highly decorated space. Less clutter means your decorations and/or collections are more visible.

What if you love every single blessed one of your 100,000 items? Hey, it could happen! Organizing allows you to store, use, and enjoy them all. Then nobody can complain, right?

Remember the whole idea of decluttering and organizing is not only to allow your unique interests and creativity to shine through, but also give you room to indulge in them if they take up space (an art room, for instance).

To that end, be not afraid to look at your rooms with new eyes. They are there to serve you, not live up to some outdated floor plan.

Non-standard Rooms

Who says the "dining room" space must be a dining room if you never formally entertain? Why not make it a library, music room, or jewelry-making room, if that speaks to your hobbies more directly? What if you had a dedicated scrap-booking area? I can see it now—tidy, gleaming, and ready for you to drop into when a spare half hour opens up.

Whenever possible, organize with a view to provide specific areas to explore your hobbies. Ready access to a good set-up increases chances of following these life-enriching interests, rather than flopping down in front of the boob tube, 'cause it's too much hassle to round up the right equipment and find a spot.

While we're at it, consider how satisfying it would be to be able to include one of those daily check-the-box memos in your calendar for spending time on your creative hobby, even if it is only thirty minutes.

It's all the rage to keep track of how many steps you walked today, or glasses of water you consumed. How much more would it refresh your life to spend a little time each day on what makes you uniquely you, an activity that speaks to your soul?

A lot, it turns out. A little time satisfying creative urges goes a long way towards making it easier to tackle the rest of the mundane day with joy and contentment.

Organizing principles

Go vertical wherever you can, i.e., get it off the floor. Think how much tidier a mop and broom look hooked into their own wall organizer than leaning dispiritedly against the wall from the floor. It gives the illusion of less clutter in your field of vision, but also takes up less floor, desk, or shelf space, allowing that feng shui energy to swirl around with abandon!

When life is in its extra-hectic stages, simplifying possessions will reduce stress. For instance, keep matching glasses in the kitchen rather than a hodgepodge of different styles. This is only an example; you may adore your hodgepodge. When there are unexpected disruptions, such as a temporary job loss or illness in the family, having an organized space (and keeping it clean) will help you feel more in control of things. Small wonder one of the first things a newly-laid-off person feels the itch to do is "finally get the closets sorted out." It is therapeutic *and* self-affirming!

At times "organizing" seems to consist of sorting belongings that have become jumbled or out of place. Just the simple act of **grouping like items and putting them away in a logical place** will give a quick sense of peace and order.

In my 7th grade home ec class, I was mesmerized by the individual tote trays we were each assigned. These kept our A-line skirt, or other sewing projects, confined to quarters between classes. During class, our tables were a mass of fabric pieces, patterns, pins, thread, and scissors. At the end of class, each student's stuff would magically get folded up and dumped into the trays, with room to spare. Instant organization and clutter-free-ness.

It was at once a lesson in the value of sorting and avoiding storage overcrowding, and given how exhilarating I found the transformation, a hint at my future.

Use your head on deciding where to **store instruction manuals**. You're unlikely to frequently need to look up how to use your refrigerator, eh? So, keep that manual in your filing system. However, if the Xbox won't cooperate, frustration will be loud and instantaneous—create a designated space close by it to store the manual.

Now you can also look up instruction manuals and user guides online, and even get a video coach via YouTube for almost anything, but if you get even more irritated not being able to pore over a paper copy, then keep them around. This is no time for over-decluttering.

Ditto when it comes to **deciding whether to keep multiples of items or just one**. You'll be surprised how much a pair of scissors and a roll of adhesive tape stored in three or four places around the house will come in handy. Keeping cleaning supplies in every bathroom reduces resistance to that dreaded chore. You'll likely only need one baby grand piano, though. See how easy that is?

Be realistic about the size of the storage space you have. It's amazing how stuck you can feel when contemplating a storage area that's full to bursting, and how it makes your whole life feel crowded.

Good for you if you've managed to pare down a quarter of your wardrobe! However, if your closet only has room for 60% of your current inventory, it's still going to look stuffed. Your choices are to create more storage (work...yuck!) or to pare down some more.

Magazine photos can be a great source of new ideas and inspiration when you see a space decorated and organized the way you want your own space to be. Post them prominently for yourself. Few things are more effective in helping you stay focused than frequently seeing your dream in front of your face.

In general, err on the side of austerity as you complete your downsizing. You'll probably be adding some things eventually...

This relates to another excellent feng shui rule-of-thumb to keep in mind: Leave at least one quarter to a third of the space open when you get each area organized to your liking, be it closet, drawer, or bookshelf. The idea is that you are energetically making room for more good things to come into your life, even if they aren't tangible items.

Storage Sucks!

I know this sounds heretical, given how much we love, crave, and fill our storage spaces. It's only the dispirited cry of a woman who sometimes assists with downsizing/packing people in preparation for a move. You've worked fingers to the bone all day long to get them ready to go, and then they remember, "Oh, yes, I also have a storage area in the basement of the building."

Makes sense it's only remembered at the last minute, since that's what we tend to do with most of the items stored in storage.

I don't judge, nor should you judge yourself, since that's what we all do with items rarely used that we can't decide what to do with. Simply keep asking whether you do truly love and use those items at least occasionally, or, you know, move them along.

Bonus Inspirational Tip

One of the all-time best methods to inspire you to shed every useless item in your house: help someone else move. Especially someone who's lived in the place for decades. You will come home determined to throw out everything you own! It's amazing how a glimpse of what others have deemed worth holding onto makes you look at your collection with brand-new eyes.

Individual Areas to Declutter and Organize

The Parking Garage

What organizing book starts with the garage? How shocking is that? For many of us, it's the family entrance to the house. What better place to start decluttering and de-stressing than the first place you see every time you come home? You could even finish the floor or walls if you go all in for that sort of thing, which might mean moving lots of things out of the space and creating the opportunity for inspection and decisions. Hmm...

It's true this may involve some negotiations if there's a man in the family who follows the trend referred to above, i.e., that men are more likely to enjoy having their possessions on display around them. At a speech I gave to an audience of primarily men I put forth my favorite solution of reducing visual clutter in the garage by storing garden tools, and even skis, upright in a large garbage bin, like a giant kitchen utensil holder.

There was a lot of disturbed murmuring in the audience, then they informed me that wouldn't work, as they all like to show off the tools and equipment they have accumulated. It's a point of masculine pride. So, be forewarned, there may be some resistance to this space-saving idea!

One great idea that did get buy-in from the whole family came from some clients of mine. They had gotten realistic about what their family really played with or used. They said the handyman supplies all perfectly arranged on the pegboard never got touched, because nowadays they always simply hired someone to fix things.

But there was an active gardener in the family, so they tossed the handyman stuff in a labeled bin and hung up the gardener's hats and tools instead.

They loved camping, skiing, and other gear-heavy pastimes, so they dedicated a big shelf with no competition from other items, located adjacent to the vehicle that gets used to take them on their adventures.

If there's a workshop area in the garage, provide it with good lighting and heat, so it's inviting to use.

Last but certainly not least, I've heard that only approximately 25% of U.S. garages have room to store the household's cars and other vehicles inside. This is because the garage often becomes a catch-all of the many items that have no other place to be stored, and/or have never had a decision made about where else to store them (or get rid of them).

This means that our (most likely) *most expensive possessions* are being left out in the rain! Good idea? Bad idea?

The Kitchen

Of all the rooms that must be kept organized as well as clean, the kitchen is right at the top of the list. Food served from a messy, dirty kitchen is unappetizing, plus keeping it clean discourages pests of the non-human variety.

In terms of decluttering and streamlining to make it easy to keep tidy, go through every gadget, fancy pan, and custom appliance you have and ask yourself if its function could easily be duplicated using some simpler item already on the "A" list in your kitchen. Try packing it away in a less prominent, but not impossible, location for six to twelve months. If you haven't really missed it, then...

Most people naturally group items for baking, food storage, drink, or snack items in their own "departments." If you are quite patient and thorough, you could even bag up the little packets you get with take-out food—mayo, ketchup, salt-and-pepper, plastic flatware in multi-packs—for the picnic department. Who knows? They might get used up that way. Or you could donate the lot to a soup kitchen.

No matter how OCD it may seem, keeping spices in alphabetical order really saves a boatload of time, not to mention allowing you to learn, belatedly, you have five jars of curry powder, when one at a time is really all you need.

Using Downsizing to Your Advantage

Once I met a woman who lived with her husband in a huge, gorgeous house, lavishly appointed throughout, except for a tiny galley kitchen inconveniently cowering in a corner, and barely big enough for one person. I asked her about it, and she said, "I really don't like people helping me in the kitchen, so I did this on purpose." She didn't say it, but I think "bothering me while I'm cooking" was another pet peeve lurking between the lines.

Have to say I'd never heard that from anyone, but if you feel that way, too, and don't have the lush budget to exclude people with architecture, you could set it up with an inscrutable logic only you can discern, and invite guests to relax in a nearby armchair. I have one in my kitchen, even though I do like assistance. Actually, I prefer sitting in the armchair and letting others do the cooking!

You can also make it easy to take advantage of guests' offers to help by having extra knives and cutting boards in a second location for a recruit to chop up veg for you.

I tend to favor simplifying the view in the kitchen as much as possible. So, I would personally steer clear of the glass-fronted dish cabinet concept (unless it has glass shelves, and translucent back lighting!). But you must please yourself on that point.

I do love a small container with spoons and other utensils handy, but only if there's some room to spare. The sight of hanging saucepans always makes me imagine a cacophony of falling pans, or heads getting conked, or worse yet, someone getting the idea that I'm so eager to cook I can't wait long enough to take a pan out of a cupboard. I wouldn't want to lie to anyone about that.

The Mailroom

Of course, dedicated mailrooms rarely exist outside corporate America, so this slightly silly designation is only thrown in to highlight the fact that some hard planning can forestall one of the most pervasive forms of clutter: piles of mail!

I recently got back on the wagon of my own policy by reinstating a paper grocery bag for recycled paper in the coat closet by the front door, which I had omitted for a while to my detriment. Now, in less than a minute and a half I can have the volume of mail down to one-quarter the original pile. Such a feeling of satisfaction to deep-six that which keeps doggedly getting sent to us without our asking, and which mostly goes in "Recycle" or "Shred."

The mailroom could be any room convenient to the mail entry point, whether office, kitchen, or laundry. It could be a small secretary table by the front door, a station in the laundry room, desk or cupboard in the kitchen, or even in your home office.

The key is making it ridiculously easy to access the second you come in the house with the mail. Reduce temptation to set it down on the counter "for now."

It's not a bad idea to put it in some visible, non-obvious place, rather than the office, where the mail could too easily get chucked and forgotten for days, as it did at mine.

I had another recycle station in my office, which seemed like a logical place, but somehow the incoming mail rarely made it there. (A matter of eight stairs and about thirty feet, and yet it couldn't seem to make that distance.) Reinstalling a recycle station by the front door instantly created a smaller mail pile instead of the usual stacks of envelopes that sat around dispiritedly for weeks.

The mailroom could have containers for recycle, shredding, trash, and depending on your temperament, one for "I don't care I promised myself to always instantly sort the mail! I don't freaking feel like it today!!" At least with the "pause" container you've kept it tidy and contained, rather than spreading all over the counter. Resolve to clear it out every 3-4 days, so it doesn't grow to an overwhelming volume.

They don't have to be dreary containers; they could be something fun like decorative magazine file holders (like cereal boxes with a slant cut through the top and down one side). Make sure the recycle one has plenty of room.

You can also use squarish baskets, inboxes, or substantial bags that will stand up by themselves (such as those you get on your glamorous shopping sprees, haha.) Make sure whatever it is, is spacious and sturdy.

Mail Stage 2

When you do feel organized enough to sort the mail from the pause container, or, you know, the actual raw pile of mail, the keepers can go into additional containers such as "time-sensitive materials," like bills and incoming checks (Hey, it could happen!), "To Read," or "To File."

If you like to get additionally streamlined, a small file box on the desk with room for just a few hanging files bridges the gap between "piles" and "out-of-sight, out-of-mind." They could have labels such as:

a. "High Priority"— Self-explanatory.

b. "Pending,"— For plane tickets, and "Waiting for info from someone else."

c. "To File"— Think twice about this one—Can you get the info again from the Internet easily? Will you ever look at it again? Could it be scanned?

d. "To Pay"

e. "To Read"

f. Other custom files for your own business or family—and even

g. "I don't know" — Get back to these when you're in a more decisive frame of mind.

This may sound a little tedious, but it does save going through a stack repeatedly, such as when you want to focus only on the bills that need to be paid shortly.

(See "More About "To File" in the home office section below.)

You can save yourself anxiety about bills/papers going out of sight into the Pending, or whatever file, by making a note in your calendar for when the bill should be paid, or the birthday card sent, or the refund applied for, and so on. (Putting stars by the time-sensitive and very important tasks helps them get done in a timely fashion. Stars even work for me!)

To reduce influx of mail:

a. Eliminate magazine subscriptions. Read online, or at the library.

b. When you order online, see if you can check or uncheck a box to avoid getting sent "offers and catalogs."

c. Go to: dmachoice.org (direct marketing association) and click on "Direct Mail 101" to get your name off lots of mailing lists.

d. Go to: optoutprescreen.com to eliminate credit card offers for either five years, or for life.

Home Office

One of my friends, who really was a tycoon for a while, was involved in three or four different business ventures. He lived in a vast penthouse apartment with windows on four sides of the building, if that gives you a vastness clue. Rather than bother with anything as plebeian as separate file cabinets for each enterprise, he simply kept the paperwork separate by having one desk per business.

This seemed like an excellent streamlining technique! But it may not be practical for your situation, so...instead, first, and foremost, make sure the office and its furnishings/décor match your personality, not somebody else's idea of how offices should look. You may spend a lot of time there; customizing it for your work style will make the time much more enjoyable and efficient.

Pare down office décor to just a few things, feng shui-inspired or otherwise, and definitely include something that makes you laugh! It may seem austere, but you'll be way more productive, relaxed, and less distracted. Think, "Tycoon-*ish*."

Get everything you use on a daily basis in your office within arm's reach. Move seldom-used manuals or other info into a different room, so you can focus on your hot projects with no dead weight around. This used to drive me crazy at various engineering jobs I had, and it eventually drove me to make darn sure all those "not-currently-needed" items were, at the very least, behind me, so I didn't even have to see them in my peripheral vision. Diva much?

More about "To File"

A fabulous, super-easy-to-use filing system is the key to not ending up with a depressing pile of "To-Be-Filed's." I like my files labeled the army way: tabs in front. That way when you pull the tab forward you are already looking at the most recent item without additional motions to get you to the front of the stack. I'm not 100% sure this is the way the army does it, but it sounds good, right?

In keeping with the "daily basis" idea above, I only keep the current or evergreen info in the nearest file cabinet or file box. Info you need to keep for a while, but may never look at again, such as tax records, goes in deep storage, elsewhere on the property (basement?) instead of taking up valuable real estate in the office.

At one time, I had my Taking Care of Business (TCB) items, like insurance and bank records, all in alphabetical order with the Fun Stuff ("House, Dream," "Restaurants to Try," etc.) and even with my consulting files. However, I could not *stand* this mixed-up set of parameters. It almost felt like my life was a jumble of nothingness as well.

Now TCB, Fun Stuff and work files are strictly separated in their own corners/file cabinets. Isn't it weird how meticulous people are about some things, and slackadaisical about others?

Make your filing system as simple as possible but still functional, and make sure it reflects your style. One of my clients felt more comfortable breaking out all her user manuals by brand name, in separate files. Fortunately, I was able to hold my tongue and not shriek, "Just throw them all in one, for Pete's sake!" as that would have been judgmental! Your call, of course.

Another client was a very sociable realtor who had earlier hired someone to set up a file system for her. It was *so* detailed that the realtor looked at the sea of files just as I would have—with complete dismay.

She was nervous about putting something in the wrong folder, with the result that the "To Be Filed" stack simply got higher and higher. I took one look at the dozens of folders and said, "Nope, we're making about eight categories out of this, so it won't be so intimidating."

I mean, who likes filing anyway? Make it as brainless as possible. Most stuff, even in the current/evergreen category, doesn't get looked at again till you do a periodic purge to the deep storage, or the shred department. It may take an extra minute pawing through the Warranties/User Manuals/Big Ticket Item Receipts file (now you see how much I combine!) looking for the fridge warranty, rather than going instantly to its exact folder. But you'll have more than made up for it with the simplicity of the filing time along the way.

If you'd rather keep all your files in one system instead of segregated like mine, you might like to color code your files. It's a very powerful tool, if you keep things simple enough to maintain easily—say, yellow for family, blue for "Taking Care of Business" (insurance, etc.), red for bills, and so on. The human eye identifies colors some orders of magnitude faster than words or numbers, so make it easy to be super-efficient that way. Plus, it's pretty!

Of course, you can also easily go paperless these days, with so much info available online, as well as the ability to scan anything paper that comes your way and store it on your computer. The IRS has long accepted scanned receipts for tax records, obviously, since you can file electronically. And, in fact, since some receipts fade over time, scanned records can be more permanent.

Seeing as how I'm a major greenie, you'd think I'd be on board with that, and I have gradually replaced several accounts' paper statements with the online kind. However, there are a few things I still like to see up close and personal, on paper. Part of this is because I spend about half my waking hours in front of a computer, so additional time there rooting out the records for Taking Care of Business (TCB) is *not* what I love. The other part is that I actually like paper and find it comforting, not to mention portable. I can study it AWAY from the blue screen!

Again, these things are individual; tailor your filing system to your liking and make that part of your life (TCB) as pleasant as it can be (reduce resistance). Accept your irrational inconsistencies, and simply do what works for you.

Bonus Tip

My Fun Stuff system includes a fat file, called "Humor," with cartoons and funny quotes in it, which I've added to for decades. If I'm feeling down, they never fail to get me laughing before long. Try as I might, I can't seem to downsize that file, as I periodically do with most folders, cuz they just crack me up every time!

The Bedroom

You've heard it before, but it's worth repeating. The bedroom is for rest and relaxation, a retreat from your hectic life. Resist the temptation to fill it with mini-home offices, televisions, PlayStations, wet bars, etc. The bedroom is the best place in the house to keep it simple.

The bedroom is also a good place to pamper yourself. One of my all-time favorite books, *Coach Yourself to Success* by Talane Miedaner, makes a very good case for going out of your way to take very good care of yourself on a regular basis, which could include a posh bedroom. By pampering yourself you gradually transform your opinion of yourself from feeling not that special (if that's where you're at), to one who feels worthy of receiving good things in this life. By seeing yourself that way, it's a short step to becoming more open to good things happening, and then to good things actually happening!

Like so many things in life, it's all a matter of attitude and taking care to see the beauty around you all the time; the beauty which may have gradually gone unnoticed in the hectic/humdrumness of everyday life (including the beauty that is you).

Give your inner interior decorator full rein in the bedroom. It doesn't take much there because simplicity is always in style. Remember how the magic of a candle can transform a room; a low-wattage lamp can do the same without putting chemicals in the air (I'm so romantic!).

Think about what helps you unwind from the day, sending you off to better sleep, and focus on those light, uncluttered touches to surround yourself with serenity.

I'll likely make some enemies with this opinion of mine, but I personally loathe having to fight my way through a baker's dozen of pillows to find the bed. What to do with them while trying to sleep? Throw them on the floor? There goes the uncluttered look! Not to mention possible danger heading for the bathroom in the middle of the night. It may be ultra-feminine and ultra-stylish, but for me it's too disconcerting to be restful. Not that we must base everything on what They say, but I haven't met one single, solitary man who likes the middle school slumber party/pillow fight effect.

OK, I'm done now.

Alas, feng shui will tell you that keeping things stored under the bed interferes with your restful sleep, and love life. If you must use that handy area for storage, try to keep it very low-key and soothing, like extra blankets and bedding—and not much of it!

In Europe, it's common to clothe a bed in a bottom sheet, pillows, and a duvet—nothing else. It's incredible how easy it is to make up the bed in the morning, and the duvet cover can be washed periodically.

Old, outdated, un-cool clothing, which has somehow shrunk in the last five years, may be gently eased out of the closet by applying the same technique mentioned above with books:

From a group of four or five garments, select the one you like the least, and put it in a separate section of your closet. Let those lesser favorites simmer for a while, or even move them to a closet far, far away in your house. See how much more vibrant your remaining wardrobe feels, and after a few days or weeks, look at the other group and see if you are not ready to move them to their next home!

More than once, I've made a conscious decision to, by golly, use all the clothes in my closet I've been neglecting. I take them in order and wear them with steely determination, whether I'm in the mood for the green-and-white striped shirt or not! Sometimes I even get creative, looking through the rest of the clothes to find different items to pair them with. What has happened the exact same number of times is that I notice I feel lackluster when I wear those clothes; it's no mystery why I've been unconsciously avoiding them.

Many clothes are kept around as echoes from a time when we weighed something different—less, maybe? Even if you do lose some of that weight, you'll be wanting something refreshingly up to date to go with your refreshed, uncluttered new attitude, am I right?

Color coding your clothes makes it easy to see how many of each color garment you have, which also makes it easier to let go of some of the over-represented tones.

    a. Some people color code by grouping all the items of one color together--easier to put coordinated outfits together in a hurry.

    b. Others group them in broad, general categories, like long-sleeve shirts, short-sleeve shirts, slacks, jackets, etc., then line up each category in rainbow order.

A big time-saver, especially if you don't tend to get your clothes very dirty over the course of your day, is to have a substantial inventory of socks and undies. Believe it or not, it is sometimes humanly possible to air out your outer garments and hang them back up, especially if your day doesn't include a lot of dirt and sweat. You wouldn't believe how long you can put off washday by doing this. (So good for the environment!)

If there's room, have a hamper for colors and one for whites, or some other division that makes sense for you.

Ever heard of this packing-for-a-trip tip? Pack one outfit for each activity anticipated, then put half of it back, and you'll usually end up with just the right amount. What if you applied that same philosophy to your wardrobe? What if you pretended you were, like, invited to stay in a castle, and, like, your luggage got lost, and you had to make do with what fit in your carry-on? I'm betting you $10 you could pick 2-3 of your all-time favorite garments, and still look fabulous all weekend. That's the magic of the favorites.

The Lounge a.k.a. The Bathroom

Consider letting each person in the family have their own color of bath towels, washcloths, etc.

(Also, each family member over the age of eight gets to learn how to do their own laundry. Not only does this teach a valuable life skill, but it also saves dozens of hours a year sorting.)

I'm not a big fan of a mishmash of bottles of products stashed anywhere and everywhere in the lounge. Try limiting yourself to only those with non-toxic ingredients. This will cut your choices down to an astonishingly small number and do your health a huge favor.

As with everywhere else in the house, an excess of stuff strewn around in the bathroom slows people down when they enter, thus encouraging a lot of dawdling in a room that, while tremendously important, is not where you want to hang out for hours.

A couple of baskets on the counter can corral a lot of small, miscellaneous items (plus, they're decorative). A little bouquet of silk flowers, a candle, or a painting helps convey the spa/vacation condo ambience, reminding us we have fun adventures to get back to.

Isn't there something about a clean bathroom sink that makes up for a lot of other lounge clutter sins? Keep a sponge or washcloth handy to wipe down the sink and faucet every day. It takes 30 seconds and pays big dividends amid the chaos.

Would you like a yummy opportunity to declutter some of your product bottles? Recently, I found the coolest shop ever for tree-huggers like me, a "refilling station." More and more cities and towns across the U.S. are sprouting stores where you can wildly expand your penchant for reducing plastic waste. Re-use trumps recycling any day, so take your empty bottles in to be refilled with everything from hand soap to shampoo to detergent to dental floss, and dozens of other products. Check this website for many resources: https://www.litterless.com/

Photo/Memorabilia "Room"

Unlike my friend, Judy, you may not have a separate room for memorabilia, but the category feels like it should have its own room, given the huge space it takes up in our hearts, heads, and houses, eh? I'm talking about the broad spectrum of photos, mementos, souvenirs, gifts, and items passed down to us from family members, whether we want them or not.

Items from the past feel comfortable because they are familiar, and sometimes they remind us of what we remember as being a good time in the past. Letting go brings up feelings of fear (See section on Fear as a Motivator in the Possessional Clutter section.), including the fear we will forget the person who gave it to us, and sometimes fear they will see that we don't have it displayed any more, causing them to become angry with us.

I had to laugh a while back, when I mentioned an item to a friend of mine that she had given me long ago. To tell you the truth, I didn't really like it that much, but I kept it, thinking she would be offended. She looked blank; clearly, she didn't remember giving it to me, as many years and hundreds of life events had happened since then.

The mother of another friend spent a lifetime impressing on her daughter the importance of keeping family antiques and furniture, taking exquisite care of those family antiques and furniture, treasuring those family antiques and furniture. After following these instructions for decades of her life (putting her own taste in décor on the back burner), my friend was more than a little exasperated when, on her deathbed, her mother said, "You know, daughter, all those antiques and furniture aren't really that important. It's the people and relationships that really matter after all."

Please let these stories be a lesson to you! And follow your own heart when deciding what to do with what other people treasure!

Photos

A few years ago, I sorted through another batch of what seemed like thousands (though probably only a few hundred) photos taken by my prolific photographer mom. These had been recently liberated due to the return to heaven of my 89-year-old stepdad. He hadn't wanted me to go through Mom's stuff too much, even though she departed nine years earlier. At first, I was sad, sad, sad, to think all those fun times they had, and how young they both looked 30 years earlier when they married. Then I thought, "Knock it off! They had a blast for 20 years, and that's life! And at least they went for the gusto!"

It was also fun to see some of the events my mom talked about, but I hadn't seen photos of, and I was fine with only keeping a representative sample.

Photos are an interesting category that may, believe it or not, shrink in future years. Now that people often take photos with their phones, yet rarely print them out, nor do anything other than store them digitally, there are likely to be millions less photos floating around in the future than there are now. Even given the fact that we probably take ten pics for every one we would have taken with our cameras (knowing the cost of getting them developed), future photo archeologists are going to have a hunt to find our photo records!

For some reason I seem to have become the storer of photos for my family, which is perfectly OK with me. **It's one of the**

categories of belongings I don't mind dedicating space to. Being a visual person, I get immense pleasure from looking at glimpses of the lives of my ancestors of the last 130 years or so (and OMG, some of those shots are like, so retro!).

Some people like to get theme books printed up for a year, or a special event, with the best photos. Or they scrapbook with photos, or get enlargements made to put up on the wall (hey, just like the old days.) I prefer storing them in photo boxes with a stack for each year (approximately). It takes up a lot less space, and someone pointed out to me that most people simply like looking at photos, whether they are in chronological order or not, and I thought, "Wow, that's right! Problem solved! Now I can store them without sweating about getting the dates perfect."

An easy way to keep the photo memories fresh is to invest in one of those digital display photo frames that shows a changing display from whatever you've stored on the disk inside. Hopefully, you've "curated" out all the ones with your thumb in the way, and where half the people have their eyes closed. Then you and the fam can enjoy them without having to delve into your phone or online archives.

Kid Art

This is a memorabilia category that can really add up, especially if parents, grandparents, or kids are very sentimental or proprietary about it. And I say, why the heck not? It's not going to fill up the basement, and eventually you will figure out a way to narrow it down. Good to have a box, perhaps the size of a larger garment box, for each child.

To encourage more artistic expression, frame up and display in a local gallery (your hallway, for instance) a unique piece from each artist.

One mom I know held that there would only be the one box per child, so each year she and the young one would decide which older pieces of art to get rid of to make room for any fantastic new ones they wanted to keep. However, if this breaks the heart of a particular child, don't be obsessive about your rule. It may truly be one of your child's burning life passions.

Maintenance

I'm bemused by the fact that I seem to let things slide, clutterwise, for a few days, just so I can have the fun of scurrying around and making it a challenge to, say, put away 50 things in ten minutes. What's that all about? I mean, I really do *love* orderly surroundings.

A kind, wise friend recently commented that such things seem to have an ebb and flow. Well, I liked that one. Instant guilt reduction, and a breath of relief. Now I feel much better about it and can actually trickle around and start picking a few things up and putting them away, since I don't have to beat myself up about it at the same time. I have an extra hand free!

The ingrained tendency to clutter up flat surfaces is a fierce one, so be prepared to come up with a strategy that works for you.

With a rare, serious warning look, my wise sister, Janice Mueller, said "Yes, it is possible to keep everything tidy all the time, but it takes CONSTANT VIGILANCE!"

Having looked back at my previous decluttering book, *100 Ways to Clear the Space for the Best of Your Life: Possessional Space*, for some clever ideas I was much struck by this tip:

> "It's inevitable, in the bustle of daily life, that things will start to pile up again. Make a pact with yourself to relentlessly keep at least a couple of areas, such as the kitchen and master bedroom, tidy. Then, at least every 3-4 days take 30 to 60 minutes to restore order in the other parts of the house, so it doesn't get away from you again."

Dang! 30–60 minutes! No wonder I'm always surprised it's such a big job when I finally get around to it. It really can be just that time consuming. Don't feel bad…And you may want to come up with an alternative approach, such as five minutes a day of order restoration in each of the main rooms of the house. You'd be staggered at how much you can accomplish in five minutes if you focus and don't dawdle.

With the rest of the family, do what you can to make the process fun, or at least highly motivated. Never underestimate the human fondness for making a game or competition out of a less than enjoyable task. It crosses all age and gender barriers, and mountains and corporations have been moved with the power of this game.

For example, leaving the TV off Saturday mornings till the kids' rooms are tidied up will ensure it gets done in record time; either that or they'll miss an entire morning of cartoons, which isn't really that bad. A friendly award or reward could be part of the program, too, such as a favorite short family outing.

Do not feel you are instilling trivial virtues in those under your jurisdiction by encouraging the spirit of self-challenge. My friend, award-winning business author, Chuck Blakeman's latest book, *Rehumanizing the Workplace by Giving Everybody Their Brain Back,* explains that incentives at work make it fun, rewarding, and profitable. He says it's substantially more powerful than simply paying people salaries for putting in their time.

On the home front, this parallels creating your own reward system to tease yourself into diving into the decluttering and organizing projects, rather than simply making yourself do it because someone told you it's a good idea.

I still never weary of the "put away 50 things in ten minutes" challenge, even if I *don't* get an ice cream cone at the end!

I once had two friends whose homes had opposite appearances. One was a harried stay-at-home mom with a 2-year-old son and an absentee husband. She had lots of stress, and lots and lots of belongings and papers spread liberally around her house. To tell you the truth, I always perceived her house as being dirty as well as messy.

The other was a recently divorced man living with his 2-year-old son, and very, very few belongings. His house seemed clean as a whistle, leaving me scratching my head, since he worked full time and didn't have a house cleaner.

One day I chanced to notice a good-sized layer of dust on the lower shelf of an end table at his house. About the same time, my woman friend told me that because of nearby construction dust constantly coming into her house, she vacuumed the house every single day.

I was blown away by the difference and tucked this maxim into my head for the long haul. **Clutter-free looks clean even when it isn't, cluttered looks dirty even when it's clean.**

Score for the person who loathes cleaning!

Stop the Clutter Before It Enters Your Domain

You may just have to be kind but firm with friends who attempt to give you their unwanted items to soothe their own guilt about the stuff. "I just don't have the room!" should be your ever-ready response. This is how the uncluttered pros do it.

Remember to take photos of your space once you get it all decluttered and organized and compare them to the ones you took when you started. Pat yourself on the back for an amazing, and often difficult, accomplishment. Also, if you like, post them somewhere to remind you of your ideal, and inspire you to restore, if necessary.

Most of all, live in the present instead of the past (too many mementos keep you anchored there) or the future ("I might need it someday"). The energy you free up by living for today will help make you more successful in every area of your life and inspire you to live the best of your life!

Bonus Tip

Your stuff's probably more than enough. If all else fails, take a leaf out of my friend's book: after a 6-week trip to Belize she came back in shock. "I thought I knew how to do without (from the way I grew up), but these people really know how to do without!" Don't underestimate your ability to improvise with what you've already got. It's better than you think.

Clutter vs. Hoarding

Who among us has not let their judgmentalness run wild with quiet glee when watching even a few minutes of a "hoarders" show? We say to ourselves, "I may be a clutterbug, but at least I'm not *that* bad!" It's way too tempting to see that practice as a personal failing among the afflicted over-savers.

So, there's a few issues tied up in that reaction.

Cluttering up is not the same as hoarding. As we've seen, cluttering is about many, many things, not the least of which is using clutter as a shield to hide our brilliance behind. "Yeah, I'd love to have some time to do [X], but the house is such a mess, I can't really do anything till I get it cleaned up…"

Hoarding, on the other hand is a hormone and/or fear-based response to not having enough, including enough love as a child in many cases. Those who hoard in a serious way have brains that temporarily or permanently see "things" differently. I once worked with a client who experienced an overwhelming series of traumas in a short period of her life which, in her case, led her to "switch over" to a hoarding response.

Her reaction was to cover every square inch of her walls with artwork, taped-up magazine pictures, letters, etc. Even though I didn't understand it on an intellectual level, I was able to put myself in her place briefly and say, "Yes, I guess if I believed bare wall meant 'unsafe,' then this arrangement would make sense."

Hoarding is an obsessive-compulsive disorder that can often be improved with the help of trained professionals. (This does NOT include wading in with a team of workers wielding dozens of garbage bags, to "get this mess handled once and for all." This may make for high-ratings TV, but it rarely provides long-term help for the person who hoards.)

Hoarding is a condition, not an identity. It certainly doesn't reflect the totality of the person. Even though those who respond to an excess of belongings in the usual way feel it must be paralyzing to be in a hoarding environment, many who hoard are able to function remarkably well in other areas of their lives, and they are often kind, intelligent people. Again, this is a result of how differently their brains view material things, not a character fault.

Hang on! Haven't I just described the truth about a lot of other conditions in life we judge people about when we don't know the whole story??

Apply the same judgmentalness decluttering to those other issues, and watch your life get simpler!

Too Decluttered?

Is it possible to pare down too much?

Yes, it is.

Whenever we ax our stuff down to the point of No-Frills Motel-ish instead of vacation condo, we can feel a little lost and not-at-home-ish, so remember to keep some remnants that define or echo your passions.

I'm not so inclined to give any pare it down to the bone photo advice. I know they're kind of an iconic memento, giving a sense of importance to some events that might have been just kind of ho-hum when the pics were snapped, but still. When one of the people in your photo collection was a great favorite person in your life and has passed away, it gives much solace to have these small mementos to return to from time to time. And, honestly, they don't take up much space, in the overall scheme of things.

This is the heart of the matter. If you get tremendous joy out of a particular activity or collection of belongings, then that's the category you don't pitch out. Simply make sure it really is one that still speaks to you, and not one you lost interest in years ago but keep around for false nostalgia. I'm going to say I feel for you if your passion is full-size sailboats, as opposed to, say, miniature antique needle-cases; you've got a big job ahead of you to accommodate that one. I'll omit "whatever floats your boat" in favor of "Better you than me, my friend!"

What's Good About Clutter?

In the spirit of first decluttering the guilts about your clutter (See Part II – Mind Clutter), consider these scenarios.

1. **Evidence of Life**: Ever been to a model home? They're always 100% clean, clutter-free, and gorgeously decorated. You can tell the designers tried hard to show "how it could really be, if you lived there," especially with the fun décor in the suggested kid's rooms! But you know with eerie certainty, even as you ooh and ahh your way through the house, that no human has ever lived there, nor ever will, in that state of endless perfection. Have any friends who keep their homes that way? Without any of the cozy clutter of human habitation, how much more than ten minutes do you really want to

spend in such a house? And do you sometimes wonder if the people who live there are actually robots??

2. **Decluttering Backfires**: Once I worked for a manager who'd taken a pricey class on how to make your business more productive (with respect to the worker bees, that is). He gave us full permission, and even the expectation, to stop work 10–15 minutes before the end of the day to tidy up our desks so we could hit the ground running next morning, unhampered by the usual disorder.

However, this had the opposite effect on me. My work was so extremely challenging and rarely enjoyable to me, that when faced with a cleared desk in perfect order first thing in the morning, my inclination was to just let sleeping dogs lie and not bother those pesky projects! It sometimes took me half an hour to get up to speed and really buckle down on their next steps. However, when I left the desk in a bit of a jumble the night before, I was much more likely in the morning to wade in with a gleam in my eye to restore order. That same 10–15 minutes of action made me feel already in motion and productive, which in turn helped me rejoin the flow of the projects and tackle the more challenging tasks.

In this way, the clutter acted as potential energy!

I've had the same experience at home. Putting away misplaced items in a small area gives enough of an energetic boost to fuel my way to faster and more widespread clearing up in the house. Before you know it, I'm ready to make that service call I've been dragging my feet on.

3. **When It Shows You're in the Flow**: OK, this is going to sound a little goofy, though men, with their enhanced ability to focus, will likely relate. What if you're right in the middle of some amazing creative project doing work you absolutely adore, and you're so in the joy of it, you don't even notice the clutter?

Once, I was so behind schedule on responding to an editor's comments on my third book that I had to ignore the sweat pouring off my body as I worked feverishly in a super-hot office in the dog days of August. I truly did not even have time to feel uncomfortable, and it didn't bother me, because I was so thrilled to near the end of the journey of getting that beloved book out into the world! I felt like the director of a blockbuster movie whose work was so "important" she couldn't possibly deign to stop and tidy things up. ("My people" will take care of it.)

The secret to that is to go ahead and set things back to rights once you finish the glorious project; otherwise you do end up getting buried in clutter. (Or, you know, get your people to do it...) For me that was the fun part, restoring order once the hard work was all done.

4. **When the Absence of Clutter Becomes the Top Priority in a Household**: When everyone in the family gets it cemented into their heads that every creative project or fun game they start will have to get completely cleared up and put away by the end of the day, that will just about be the end of any creative projects or fun games being started. You'll have a perfectly orderly home with a lot of TV or video game watchers in it. Or you'll have a frequently empty house, because those who

gravitate towards more relaxed surroundings will leave it as often as they can.

You don't want that, do you? I didn't think so.

Decluttering is Transformative

My whole life I have been thrilled to hear the stories of unfortunates nearly swallowed up in clutter being rescued by various angels of organizing coming into their homes and transforming them into visions of cleanliness and order.

It started in Brownie Scouts. We learned the story of the Brownies, magical creatures who came in while some poor, overwhelmed widower was off earning the family's daily crust. For whatever reason, his children couldn't be bothered to help out around the house at all. Enter the Brownies, who completely cleaned up the house, laid a fire, and left a meal on the table, like magic! Once the children saw how relieved and loved it made their father feel to come home to this, it inspired them to start pitching in. We were encouraged to be similarly helpful. I never stopped adoring that story, no matter how many times I heard it.

Clearly, I'm not the only one, or we wouldn't have the massively popular TV shows about not just decluttering but also home remodeling makeovers. What is it that makes these stories so magical? To me they are much more compelling than simply designing a great new space from the start.

Why are we drawn so much more poignantly to the stories of the ugly becoming beautiful? I don't know the whole answer to that, but I think it has to do with one of the oldest stories in the world: the story of transformation, the lost becoming found again, the resurrection of our very souls. Wow! No wonder it's nearly irresistible to long for that for ourselves.

PART IV
CLEAR THE BODY CLUTTER

The wise Zen words on page 1 sum up the joy of clearing physical body clutter:

"How refreshing is the whinny of the pack horse relieved of all burden."

I can personally vouch for this joy, thanks to my first and most miserable backpack trip, made at age fourteen. I had half-heartedly trained at sea level in coastal California with a 27-pound pack for about a mile each evening before gratefully dropping the pack, and myself, in front of the TV. Imagine the shock when I went off to hike in the Sierra Nevada Mountains. We started at 8,000 feet elevation and went up from there, eventually to 11,000 feet.

The true horror of the situation hit me at the end of the first mile. I gratefully shed my now-32-pound pack for a rest, then, if you follow me closely, instead of watching TV till bedtime… we put our packs back on and started walking again, many more miles that day. Not to mention having to set up tents, find firewood, and cook supper.

A week, and dozens of freeze-dried meals later, we headed back out. I was down to 18 pounds in my pack since much of the original 32 pounds was food. And this horsey nearly skipped all the way back to the barn, delirious with the joy of a lighter load, a return to non-powdered food, and torture's end in sight!

The clutter of the physical body may be easy to identify, such as some extra weight you would, however reluctantly, be willing to part with, or they may be in small bits throughout your body that add up to a lot of burden, like arterial plaque.

But as we've said, not for the first time, physical body clutter doesn't impact only your body. Your emotions droop with the weight of them, and your initiative to downsize your stuff can feel equally depleted.

On top of this temporary dreariness is the long-range fact that physical body clutter carried year after decade contributes significantly to the degenerative diseases widespread among us. Not to mention the acceptance that these diseases are an inevitable part of aging. Poppycock!

Many, many degenerative diseases can not only be prevented by decluttering the body, but in some instances, they can even be, to some extent, reversed. That's how versatile our bodies are.

The good news is people are waking up to that fact, with the result that many people are living longer, healthier lives, and then departing this life suddenly, rather than languishing in nursing homes for years. Who doesn't like that idea, given the options?

The Electric, Scintillating You

I must tell you, I was so in awe of how dazzling our bodies are, I nearly subtitled this book *Declutter Body, Mind, and Stuff: Discover the Electric, Scintillating You!*

Close call! (Had to recalibrate when one of my test audience members said "What's 'scintillating'?" and another said the very thought made her tired.)

But if we could, just for a moment, think about electric/scintillating, what if we took a giant step up to the well-known 50,000-foot level? From there, it's easier to see ourselves clearly and appreciate the glorious beings we truly are!

Remember what happens in your brain when you mentally start moving out, from ground to stratosphere to solar system to galaxy to universe—you could hear a pin drop inside that brain as you contemplate the wonder of it.

The same thing happens when you think about what actually goes on inside your body. Looking progressively inward reveals another astonishing world—from skin to internal organs to cells to subcellular constituents to molecules to quarks (energy)...How extraordinary it is!

On a strictly physical level, recall from high school biology, that you're made up of some 30-40 trillion cells, all working together in a dazzling fashion to keep you functioning more or less like clockwork, for up to 52,560,000 minutes in a row (if you live a hundred years). Even if it's less years, it's still a lot of minutes for this organism to perk along.

The body is said to perform about 15,000 chemical reactions/second, between respiration, digestion, elimination, and the other X number of functions our bodies do. I've heard it said the average human body has enough energy tied up in it (think $E = mc^2$) to power a city of 60,000 for a week. That's a lot of electricity...

Holy cow! You're amazing!

As my high school biology class friend, Eric Dietrich, said when my eight-month-old reached his hand out, "I'd love to have the software for that." He was investing in artificial intelligence at the time; now he's a professor of philosophy. He tells me we still know vastly more about astronomy than how human bodies and brains work.

If this sounds a little high-flown, you are seriously underestimating yourself; our bodies are truly remarkable!

What's this got to do with decluttering? Only a little reality check to generate some enthusiasm for taking care of your gorgeous physical body home!

By the way, if you need more ammunition to admire how unique you are, check out this nice reminder from Barry Overton, author of *Ignite Your Greatness: The Secret to Lighting the Fire Within*. Overton explains just what a miracle, in statistical terms, it is that each of us is born exactly as we are. From the odds of our parents actually meeting each other in this world once (1 in 20,000) to them getting to the point of baby-making (1 in 2,000), to the fact that 1–2 million potential eggs in a young woman's body reduce down to only about 400 eggs that are stored for use, to the millions of sperm that could have done the job of fertilizing the egg, but only one does.

Bottom line: the odds of the actual you, me, or anyone else being born is about one in 400 trillion. So, you're very special!

Why Physical Body Clearing Matters So Much

Why am I so all-fired-up about detoxing your bod?

A piece of research that blows me away each and every time I think about it, inspired this section of *Clear the Space, Feel the Rush*, and always inspires me to do some body detox:

At the Rockefeller Institute, chicken cells were kept alive for 34 years by simply cleansing the wastes away each day. No meds, no surgery, no therapy, just keepin' it clean.

The primary reason they finally died was because someone inadvertently omitted the cell cleansing for a few days. Those cells weren't exposed to much in the way of toxins, so it was their own waste products that did them in.

Adding to the wastes generated in our own bodies, there are chemicals all around us: in the air, in our homes and workplaces, and unfortunately, also in the processed foods we eat. Just as the clutter in our homes creeps up slowly, the cumulative effect of hundreds of meals that include non-food items gradually saps our energy and vitality.

Remember the rush you get from a good declutter-your-stuff day? Decluttering your body has the same exhilarating effect, though the effect may take a bit longer (apart from the fast rush from exercising).

This small-but-mighty point is important to keep in mind. You can mess up your whole house in far less than a day and put it back to rights in a day or a few days.

Because your body is always working away at detoxing you, it may take several years before the cumulative effects of eating junky food or not exercising impact your health. The good news is it doesn't take years to undo it all!

A meal of primarily uncluttered, energy-giving foods, will leave you feeling better than one that's 100% "junk" food. A fifteen-minute walk, or a do-it-yourself yoga session, or ten pushups, perks the body up.

It may take a couple of weeks of eating better or exercising more regularly to feel better more consistently. It may even take a few months to get there.

This process is more gradual, so be patient with yourself— the results are worth it!

Decluttering your body (detoxing) is as much of a rush as decluttering your home. Your emotions, as well as your physical self, feel lightened and energized.

Disclaimer

As a professional nutritional counselor, physical trainer, wellness practitioner, or what-have-you, I make a great engineer. This is because I may have studied these topics in *excruciating* detail for years, but I don't consider myself an expert qualified to make specific recommendations for two simple reasons:

1. Generally accepted "wisdom" (science, research, opinion) about "the best thing to do for the body" seems to change about every three weeks, so there's no way to keep up with that roller coaster. (Only a slight exaggeration.)

2. It's truly mind-boggling how different bodies react to the same nutritional/kinesthetic stimuli. It's simply not possible to accurately predict the outcome of a given exercise or diet.

You may feel the sun rises and sets in the weight room, that there's nothing better than blastin' through 20 reps with barbells hanging off every limb 6 hours a week, while others revel in a relaxing hour of yin yoga.

(Should you wonder what yin yoga is, picture the most relaxing yoga poses you can, held for 5 minutes or more each. Let yourself succumb to gentle music and a whisper-smooth instructor's voice, and this class will make your blood sing, I promise you! Who'd have thought?)

I've also done the weight-lifting routine, and for me, the blast is in how you feel when you're through with the workout. But during? Not so much.

Similarly, for you, three doughnuts a day may be just the thing to keep the doctor away, and that spring in your step, but others may prefer to forego doughnuts altogether, in favor of radishes, radicchio, red beans, and rice. Strange, but true…

Therefore, we're sticking with general guidelines and reasons for clearing the physical body space, and leaving the details up to you and your health care practitioner, exercise coach, personal trainer, etc., etc.

Cleansing – Body Detox

You might be thinking, "Hey, why should I detox? I eat vegetables occasionally! I don't smoke crack!"

With all the hype about the importance of doing cleanses these days, it's reassuring to know a respectable percentage of those 15,000 chemical reactions per second mentioned above have to do with elimination of wastes. In other words, detoxifying. Your body is amazing in what it can detoxify, and it's on the job 24/7.

This is all good, otherwise, you wouldn't still be here.

However, the load can be heavy, depending on where you live and breathe.

Estimates of the number of chemicals used in the U.S. commerce vary widely, but a conservative number is around 9,000. Hard to know how many chemicals people are exposed to daily, but few of them are likely to be what our bodies were designed to absorb. Obviously, they're very, very adaptable, but there's no denying they could use a little help.

Our bodies don't know what to do with all those processed food chemicals, on top of the other chemicals we come in contact with, so they just sit around in our bodies waiting for a clean-up crew—which is us!

Many systems and organs have a hand in keeping things clean on our insides, but the heaviest hitters are liver, kidneys, lymphatic system, and excretory system (colon, bladder, etc.) Lungs and skin are more on the protection side of things, preventing the world from detoxing itself into you!

Liver

The liver has over 500 functions, many of which involve removing toxins from our body. It's the first place everything we eat, drink, breathe in, or absorb through our skin goes to for removing toxins, if needed. When the number of toxins into your body exceeds what the liver can excrete, they end up being stored there. A "dirty" liver contributes to a staggering number of negative conditions, from allergies, to moles, to jaundice, to liver failure and, you know, death, in extreme cases, especially when an ocean of alcohol has streamed through you.

OK, we're probably not at that point, but a lot of us care when that most cosmetically important one is impacted: fat loss. If the liver keeps getting fed junk or processed food, it will shut down any activities for ridding your body of excess fat in order to get rid of those chemicals first. This is why the fast-food diet doesn't work for weight loss, unfortunately.

Eating a low-processed-food diet goes a long way helping your liver do its job easier, but you can assist with a low-tech liver cleanse: drink a tablespoon or so of fresh organic lemon juice in a small glass of warm or cool water first thing in the morning.

To supercharge that liver cleanse, add a drop each of therapeutic- or premium-grade peppermint and lemon essential oils. Wait at least 20 minutes before you eat. (See section below in "Medicine Cabinet" section about essential oils, as not all are equal, especially when it comes to ingesting them. If you can't get therapeutic-grade essential oils, then simply use the lemon juice.)

Bonus Tip

With or without the essential oils, you can turn the liver cleanse into an easy winter detox and immune builder. Add a pinch of cayenne pepper to warm you up and get rid of mucus. It's said to be a blood purifier, too. Each day increase the amount of cayenne pepper, if you can stand it, up to a teaspoon or so, for more benefit. Then there's a teaspoon of honey that can be added for improving coughs and sore throats. This liver cleanse starting to sound not too bad!

There are other ways to clean the liver, too, including recommended products at a reputable health store. This is one of those topics it is better for you to research for yourself. **And to repeat, the best liver detox is in cutting down on toxins in.**

Kidneys

Your kidneys receive blood from the liver, which has broken down any poisons to less-toxic substances. The kidneys send those substances to be excreted in urine or feces. Both exercise and drinking enough water (covered below) help the kidneys do their vital job.

Lymphatic system

Like the bloodstream, the lymphatic system plays a huge role in keeping our bodies clean and healthy. While blood brings nutrients and water into the cells, the lymph circulatory channels bring that water and the cell's waste products back to a different area of the bloodstream to be filtered through liver and kidneys and sent out the door.

Unlike the bloodstream, lymph doesn't have its own pump (heart), but instead is moved by our movements, which is one of the many reasons exercise or simply moving the body are so important.

Bladder

The bladder is a star that keeps doing its detoxing function of getting rid of fluid waste from your body without a lot of interference. You can keep it happy by keeping its musculature in good shape and taking in enough water.

You do the first by urinating at least once every 3-4 hours rather than holding on endlessly. For many that's a laughable stat since we tend to urinate far more often. Imagine my surprise recently to learn that going too often, and especially going "just in case" before you head off on a journey that will keep you away from the bathroom maybe a little too long, is just as non-helpful, as it tends to weaken the bladder's muscles by never challenging them at all.

Kegel exercises (purposely tensing pelvic floor muscles for a few seconds, then releasing) have long been recommended to keep that area in good shape and prevent embarrassing leaks, however lots of confusion has been introduced in recent years about what is the "correct" way to them.

The real story was cleared up for me in one sentence recently when a nurse I know said "The muscles that matter [for reducing the threat of incontinence] are the ones that control the urine flow, not necessarily all the muscles in the pelvic floor."

So, there it is in one. Go ahead and do your Kegels if you like, but give the bladder muscles the workout they can use by practicing starting and stopping the flow of urine while you are urinating.

The question of how much water to drink daily has been debated endlessly. Yes, you can overdo it, but it's super hard to do. Most of us err on the side of dehydration. With enough water in our bodies, brains work better, skin is softer, and pain is reduced. Did you know drinking water is the fastest way to reduce headache pain?

Realizing the average adult excretes about two cups of water a day just through normal respiration, and a total of eight cups between breathing, urination, and sweating combined, puts the recommended 8-12 eight-ounce glasses of water a day in perspective. That's 2-3 quarts a day. Adding a physical workout increases that water loss from your body. Easy to see why many of us are considered constantly dehydrated.

How is it we haven't dried up and blown away with all the days we didn't remember to drink that much H2O? The good thing is it doesn't all have to be straight water, since almost all foods have water content, especially fresh fruits and vegetables. Any beverage or food item not containing alcohol or caffeine will help your hydration level go up.

And your urine gives you a super-easy way to tell if you are or aren't getting the right amount of water intake. If it's bright yellow, you're not getting enough, light yellow, just right, colorless, maybe too much. This may even be a better indicator than simply going by thirst, as we don't always pay enough attention to that to notice, especially if we're not used to tuning in closely.

By the way, not only the bladder, but all these organs and systems discussed above plus the ones below, plus the whole rest of your body love it when you provide enough water!

Side note: Like many, I was eager to believe the idea it would help flush out my kidneys by making sure I drank those 8-12 cups in addition to what I ate. Imagine my surprise to learn our entire blood volume (roughly 5-7 quarts) filters through our kidneys dozens of times a day, a total of 150–200 quarts! So, um, sounds like they're getting pretty flushed out anyway...

Colon

Skipping nimbly right past any stupid clichés about the bottom line in body detoxifying, let me say that a colon cleanse pulls it all together in the body detox department. If every other bodily part gets the cleanse and that one doesn't, then there's no place for junk to go. Because of this, some people start here and work their way up the system.

The traditional American diet of meat and potatoes, plus dairy and sugar, low in the fiber/fruit/veg line, can reduce the colon's ability to clear itself out, contributing to constipation. It's not unknown to have many pounds of impacted material (remaining nameless) sitting there around our middles, adding to the appearance of obesity and making us feel sluggish.

All kinds of colon cleanses are the rage these days, and some are pretty extreme. One surprising and happy fact is that we can get excellent results at pulling out deep-down, years' old toxins from our colon with more gradual cleanses that include herbs. Experts warn cleanses that include ingredients such as clay or large amounts of psyllium husk, for example, may be themselves providing some of the material that comes out the other end, making us think we're really releasing more than is actually in there. The herbal cleanses bypass this possibility.

Again, I'm going to defer to the experts on this, and simply recommend the practice. Find a regimen you can stick with and go for it. There are numerous good herbal cleansers to be found at a health food store or through a nutritionist. It takes about thirty days to get 'er done, and then you repeat every year or so to keep lively. As it works its way up your system, after a week or two, the strange things that emerge from you will make you a believer that they are worth getting rid of.

The important thing to remember is to keep eating whatever fruits, vegetables, or other high-fiber foods you were already eating, so your body doesn't come to rely too much on the herbs for elimination. Cut back on the cleanse if needed, rather than the fiber foods.

It's not always a pleasant process, but there are few things that will make you feel friskier (and you may even lose a few pounds without effort) than a colon cleanse. Remember those chicken cells...

You can also help your body detox by not only eating certain high-fiber foods to help it clear out, but by making new eating decisions to avoid building up body junk in the first place (See the "Eat!" section below.)

Foods that help detox your body have soluble and insoluble fiber. My eyes are starting to cross already, with the thought of more know-how/decisions required, but it's really not that complicated.

Most fruits, vegetables, and grains have both types of fiber; some have higher percentages of one over the other. All fiber can improve gut health, help control blood pressure, and lower the risk of diabetes, as well as colon and breast cancer.

Soluble fiber foods, such as plant pectin, dissolve in water. Whole grains such as oats and barley, as well as vegetables (peas, carrots) and fruits, especially citrus fruits and apples, as well as psyllium, are higher in soluble fiber, which helps the body improve glucose regulation, in addition to the benefits mentioned above.

Insoluble fiber foods do not dissolve in water and are traditionally what was known as "roughage." Part of the fiber is indigestible and serves merely to help the digestive waste material through, when combined with water. Foods high in insoluble fiber include cruciferous vegetables (broccoli, cabbage, and kale), nuts and seeds, wheat bran and whole wheat flour, and green beans.

Finally, beans, sprouted grains (available in commercially baked bread), and prunes are high in both types of fiber.

With diets high in refined flour and sugar, many Americans run short on the recommended 25 grams of fiber a day. However, it's not as hard as it might seem. Including high-fiber cereal for breakfast, making sure each meal has 1-2 servings of fruits and vegetables, and including beans (nachos count!) a few times a week can make the transition easy.

If you haven't eaten much fiber before, increase the amount slowly, and include plenty of water to help the fiber do its job.

Lungs

The lungs have 600–800 square feet of surface area to receive oxygen and discharge carbon dioxide from our bodies. They also work to filter toxins we breathe in, collecting them in mucus, which we cough or sneeze out, preventing them from entering our bodies in the wrong places.

The reason smoking or living with a lot of pollution is so hard on your lungs is that they coat that huge area with tar and other sludge, more than what the filtering function of the lungs can handle. This reduces oxygen in, so your body works less efficiently (polite term for increased weakness and sickness.)

Anytime you exercise you help the efficiency of the lungs to bring oxygen into your body. It's tempting to think exercise is beneficial for removing the waste gas – carbon dioxide, but the truth is when you exercise, you also increase the production of CO_2, so the net result stays the same. However, the exercise does help the oxygen exchange become more efficient, because, let's face it, if you're exercising, you're likely breathing deeper, and that's where the payoff comes from.

Deep breathing (involving the whole lungs, all the way down to the bottom of your abdomen) is even better. For one thing when you breathe to the bottom of your lungs (diaphragmatic breathing) more of your body is in motion helping the lymph system do its work. For another, when you don't use your diaphragm much to breathe, then other muscles in neck, shoulders and chest have to fill in, and oxygen intake is less efficient that way.

For years I believed toxins are shed when we exhale, but when I looked for scientific evidence of it, I didn't find much, other than during certain severe illnesses, and/or when we're breathing the same toxins in, so some of them come back out, as with smoking.

Deep breathing is what babies do automatically, but as we get older, we tend to breathe higher and higher in our chests, that is, shallower and shallower, a perfect example of mind-body interactions. The older we get, the more cautious and fearful we may become, and we hold our bodies increasingly still. Declutter the fears (mind clutter), and the breathing becomes deeper and more relaxed, too. Breathe more deeply and the mind becomes more relaxed. Nice how that works!

Although they may or may not help you detoxify your lungs, certain essential oils can help you breathe easier when you've had an allergic-type response that shortens your breath. This is done through diffusing and/or inhaling. Believe it or not, that goopy stuff Mom put on your chest when you had a cold that made your eyes water and your teeth curl has eucalyptus and mint essential oils in it. Diffusing essential oils is one of the thriftiest uses of them, as it breaks down the drops into hundreds of smaller particles, which spread out on the lung's large surface.

Herbs can also help clear out the lungs, and I must leave that to the herbalists, as it exceeds my knowledge base. Suffice it to say many herbs contain essential oils, much more spread out among the dry plant matter, so less concentrated. Your body might prefer it.

The good news is lungs are extremely resilient, eliminating the toxins you breathe in (this is code for "stop smoking" or "change your environment to lower air pollution") and they will gradually clear themselves out, to the extent they can, unless permanent damage has occurred.

Skin

Skin is the body's largest organ, a fact which tickles me, since we usually think of it only in cosmetic terms. It covers about 22 square feet and makes up a little over 15% of our weight. According to the American Academy of Dermatology (AAD) we're also shedding about 30,000–40,000 skin cells a day. It's easy to see how this could mount up over time. It comes out to about 9 pounds a year!

Its main job, other than keeping our insides inside, is protection from outside toxins.

This is why bathing is so excellent for health—it washes away those skin-blocked toxins before they can worm their way inside you. Again, I had long been led to believe toxins were excreted from the skin, along with our sweat, but that's another tale that may only sound good, rather than be true.

Still, bathing is good, and not only for improving your smell! Just because I don't like getting wet doesn't mean anything. Too bad Mom didn't convey this factoid when I was growing up. She would have had an easier time of it.

It's easy to laugh about bathing, but what does it do for our skin, declutter-wise?

1. Removing toxins and dirt, obviously.
2. Adding moisture to the skin. According to an esthetician friend, only about 5–10% of the water we drink makes it as far as the skin. The skin moisturizing effect of bathing extends to hair and eyes as well.
3. Washes away dead cells which can become inflamed.
4. If you take an actual bath, rather than a shower, the warmth of the water causes blood vessels to dilate, lowering blood pressure. Regular use of baths has been shown in studies to reduce risk of heart attack and stroke by about 25%. (If you already have low blood pressure, use caution with baths, saunas, and hot tubs. Get in slowly to allow your body to acclimate, and limit time in the water, especially if you feel lightheaded.) Yay! Now I

can say the whirlpool/hot tub at my pricey athletic club has health benefits!

Also, have you ever noticed how good you feel when you get the right amount of exercise (bringing out the endorphins), and head out from a nice, hot shower? It isn't just the joy of the workout being over, it's the invigorating effect of clean skin! (I bet.)

That old line "you are what you eat" should be expanded to include "you are what you absorb." This includes everything you put on your skin, which I understand is also on its way to your (possibly) overtaxed liver in thirty seconds.

As with food labels, ingredient lists on skin care products can be confusing. For example, the ominous-sounding "Butyrospermum parkii" is actually a now-replaced name for shea butter, harmless to skin and you. (New name is *Vitelleria paradoxa*, but doesn't the old one sound scarier?) Companies specializing in non-toxic skin products will have lists online of ingredients to avoid.

The top 18–23 layers of our skin consist of dead cells, which is where those 30,000–40,000 cells a day comes from.

Exfoliating can help remove the top layer of that dead skin more efficiently, resulting in brighter-looking skin and better absorption of topically administered medicines. Long-term use can result in increased collagen production, for younger-looking skin. Score!

However, the American Academy of Dermatology advises caution regarding how often and what type of products to use, because their effects vary based on skin type. Check their website for more info: aad.org.

Does the thought of actively exfoliating simply make you tired? As in, "Really? One more thing I have to do?" The answer is no. Your skin will keep ditching those 30–40K cells a day no matter what. Plus, for some people, exfoliating can do more harm than good, causing redness and worsened acne! So, hey, feel totally free to assume you're one of those people, and skip this time-consuming step…

Uncluttered Food

Don't Be This Guy – The Bachelor Fridge

Years ago, company was coming over, so I cleaned out my fridge, which happened about as often as the national budget gets balanced. Once the ancient foodstuffs clad in molds of many colors were disposed of, what was left was a lot of condiments, a six-pack of beer laid in against the expected company, and one of my roommate's leftover pizza boxes.

I was struck by the picture of perfection it made:

The Essential Bachelor Fridge!

No space wasted kowtowing to the Nutrition God! I mean, who made up that garbage about "five servings of fruits and vegetables a day," anyway?! Five servings are more than plenty for a year! All the basic junk food groups, fat, salt, and sugar (alcohol) were represented, except caffeine. But, not to worry…the caffeine was in the programmable coffee-maker ready to create breakfast, so—handled!

Clean, uncluttered, organized…hmmm.

At the age of twenty I had a watershed moment understanding just how strongly non-food chemicals impact our bodies. A summer job practicing engineering had me working with a couple construction workers building concrete footings for a mobile classroom. The footings, which were meant to hold up the building, were basically rectangular troughs in the ground; they were about two feet deep, two feet wide, and 15–20 feet long. My job was to run a basic survey instrument and check that the tops were level when they got to that point.

As soldiers speak about wartime--months of boredom followed by moments of terror and, uh, high engagement—thus was my job of waiting to survey the footings, i.e., their work took lots more time than mine. First the holes had to be dug, then gravel shoveled in the bottom a few inches deep, then the concrete poured in. After two days of desolate boredom, I begged them to let me help. At first, they only let me pick up the random shovels or rakes left on the wrong side of a trench they were working on, but they finally relented and let me do some of the physical labor.

After a life led as close to sedentary as possible without being actually deceased, I only lasted two hours the first day. I was able to work four hours the next day, and by the third day, I worked the whole eight hours. Suffice it to say I was working at my peak strength at that time, coming home thrillingly exhausted with the satisfaction of having put in a good, hard day's work. I was oddly less hungry than usual, but the key difference I noted was that there was no way I could face drinking a diet soda those nights, as I normally did occasionally. Just the thought of it made my stomach turn.

"Hmm," I thought, "Here's my body, working at its peak performance, and it is rejecting the chemically enhanced drink on no uncertain terms. Could that chemical be, perchance...toxic to me?" My brain was able to extrapolate out with the novel thought that maybe some other food chemicals could also be rejected by my bod when it was speaking very plainly from its high-performance wisdom.

As per now-common advice, a super-easy way to keep unwanted chemicals out of your food is to stick to the aisles around the perimeter of the grocery store (not counting the pharmacy and Styrofoam coolers sometimes located there) Thus, cleverly circumnavigating the store, you find foods with only one ingredient, like "blueberries," for instance, rather than "blueberry toaster pastry," or eggs, or walnuts.

Not only do you declutter your diet of unwanted chemicals, but you also prevent extra packaging from entering your life and needing disposal. This is because the one ingredient foodstuffs don't need to be labeled or embalmed, i.e., preserved.

The middle aisles tend to be stocked with processed foods, which often have staggeringly long ingredient lists. Occasionally, a couple of those ingredients might actually be vitamins with foreboding-sounding names. But most are not; they're either used for keeping the foods stable for eternity, giving them a more acceptable texture, helping keep us addicted to the food, or who knows what. They may be harmless, but they still take up needless, unfulfilling space in your tummy, giving nothing to nourish you, and creating more work for your hard-hitting liver.

Eat!

Declutter the idea that starving yourself is cool, or in any way worthwhile.

Ever hear about that starvation experiment they did during World War II with a group of conscientious objectors who volunteered for the project? The idea was to study what effects the starvation treatment prisoners of war would be experiencing in the Far East at that time. The volunteers agreed to consume just half the normal number of calories per day for six months.

They started out joking and talking with each other, playing cards, and generally enjoying themselves and others. But as the weeks went by, they all became progressively more sullen, antisocial, prone to anger, erratic, and even psychotic. One man cut off three of his own fingers in his extreme distress. The mental and emotional effects of the malnutrition lasted beyond the end of the experiment.

A horrific story, but did you ever stop to think what the long-term effects on your health are if you've, say, skipped a meal every day all your life 'cause you just don't feel like eating in the morning, or you're too busy, or you think it's cool, or you think it's a good way to lose fat, or you'd rather drink your dinner?

If you can honestly say your brain and body function at their peak while you refuse/forget to refuel them, then you are kidding yourself. Your brain uses 25% of your calories, and if your blood sugar is at a low ebb for a significant chunk of the day, guess what suffers first? (Hint: not rocket science.)

Those feel-good brain chemicals like serotonin (what antidepressants are supposed to keep up) also need proteins, fats, and carbs to be produced in your body. When you're feeling extra-grumpy, it's possible malnutrition is playing a part.

At the extreme end of that spectrum, did you know chronic food deprivation may contribute to dementia? Three squares a day might be cool after all.

I am no purist shaking an admonishing finger at you from the top of a perfection mountain, so fear not the judgment. It's always an ongoing project, and luckily, as stated before, our amazing bodies give us a lotta, lotta chances.

They say Americans have the best opportunity to enjoy a fantastically varied diet, yet most consume the least varied diet in the world. I had a friend once who bragged about how he ate the same lunch every day for years, one piece of fruit (the same one) and one semi-vegetable (the same one.) He thought he was showing admirable restraint and healthiness due to his natural lunch fare. I gave him the raspberry, which he should have eaten, too, then he'd at least have three items on the menu instead of two!

Eating a wide variety of foods means you get the best shot at getting more of your nutrients from real food, which, despite the wonders of supplements (see below), is still the best way to get them. That's because whole foods have synergistic chemicals (nutrients) in them that help with nutrient absorption.

According to Ayurvedic medicine (ancient wisdom from India), our bodies do their most excellent digestive work between the hours of 10 am and 2 pm, so technically, lunch could/should be the most beneficial time to eat your biggest meal, not breakfast. Sorry, Mom, and about a million other advice givers.

The main thing is to supply our bodies with enough fuel to keep consistently nourished, in about 3 meals a day (not 6 or 10, just 3—constant snacking messes with the work of your digestive system, and your body's internal processes with insulin and blood sugar).

But what if the last thing anyone could accuse you of is undereating? What if those three squares a day have lots of company, and you still feel the brain and body tottering around on about three cylinders?

Look at what you are eating. If it includes lots of junk food, fast food, pre-packaged food, or a very limited variety, you could still be suffering from malnutrition, believe it or not. Key trace minerals, also needed in that all-important serotonin production, are usually missing from all the above. You keep eating and eating in a desperate attempt to get what your body needs, and it never gets supplied, so you continue to feel hungry and blue.

It's worth repeating from above that junk/fast/pre-packaged food gets in the way of dropping unwanted pounds. With your liver's number one function being detoxifying, it must shut down more glamorous activities you might prefer, like burning off extra fat, until all the toxins are processed, neutralized, and vaporized, or whatever happens in there.

Bottom line, I'm not a nutritionist, nor a dietitian. I just know what I see, with people ignoring their beautiful bodies' need for some good stuff to eat.

To keep up your energy and your competitive edge, these tips will serve you well:

- Eat the biggest variety of food you can think of, especially vegetables and fruit.

- Eat the simplest version of each food—for example fresh cherries, instead of packaged cherry Danish.

- Eat at least a little protein at every meal. It doesn't have to be big, just give your body something to work with, like a boiled egg, or a handful of almonds. If you can't choke down even that much sustenance, plug your nose and chug a 30-second protein smoothie. There is protein in most foods, except fruits, so the bar is not high to get that protein into you.

- Find creative ways to enjoy foods other than those that feature high amounts of sugar or flour. Despite being "a single ingredient," these sneaky foods are already highly processed and refined, so they don't help your cause at all. They disrupt your blood sugar, and unlike slower-absorbed carbs, contribute to arterial plaque, and a host of degenerative diseases. You already know by now it wasn't the fat after all, right? And it wasn't the cholesterol either! It was the simple carbs, in excess, all along!

What I Learned from a Vegetarian Wrap:

Once I was running late, a completely rare occurrence, of course (not), for a large seminar, where boxed lunches were being provided. Since I also hadn't specified my lunch choice ahead of time, the vegetarian wrap was the only option left. So, I took a vegetarian wrap lunch box, thinking, "OK, I guess there'll probably be some cheese in it, or something, for vegetarian."

Imagine my immense surprise to learn that, no, it was a tortilla filled with…vegetables! No cheese, no tofu, just veg. Might have been some avocado or mushrooms, I don't remember, and there was plenty of filling, plus my choice of mustard or mayo to add, but yep, only vegetables.

The other thing that was super-surprising was how awake and energized I felt all afternoon. No temptation to doze off in the boring bits of the seminar. No flagging of energy. Just a constant ability to brightly fake interest in the words droning out.

"So," I thought, "This is what they mean by energizing-foods-not-with-caffeine!" That's the ATP cycle of cell energy when your cells' mitochondria take food and oxygen and fire out energy. It's the most natural form of energy for people.

I still think it's valuable to eat some dense protein with most meals, but this experience, which I wouldn't have voluntarily undertaken, was a real eye-opener for me.

Healthy food may not make you a million bucks, but it will keep the brights on in your brain and mood, and also potentially help you preserve your own health, which is worth at least $1 million, I'm thinking!

And Water, Declutter Those Bottles of

Being a hard-core conservationist, I've been anti-bottled water since day one. It's not enough that they fill up landfills and lakes, to discourage people from using them, then there's how much water it takes to produce a bottle of water (3-5 gallons, including what it takes to make the plastic!).

The evidence against them seems to be accelerating. Compare the cost to consume a years' supply of all that recommended 8-12 glasses a day via bottled water ($2500) versus tap water (at about $1)! And that the two biggest bottled water producers are merely giving us filtered tap water, not the crystal-clear spring water we dreamily imagine it to be. And the most hilariously ridiculous fact of all? Federal standards for bottled water are less stringent than for tap water! HAHAHAHAHA.

I know, I know—some tap waters taste blech, depending on where you live, and can have some ingredients that you don't want in them. Your best bet is to find a filtering system you like and run your tap water through it. Save the bottled water for extreme situations, of which, you know, there really aren't that many.

Dieting – A Good One to Let Go Of

Diet:

Eat more vegetables.

Exercise.

Ever notice how most diets, specifically weight-loss programs, narrow down to one or both of these instructions, at the bottom line? (Unless they also include "Consume my expensive, but perfect weight-loss supplement!")

Weight loss (code for "extra fat reduction," not just any old body weight reduction): We both know there are hundreds of theories, products, and methods all claiming to be "the one" you need to drop the excess, unneeded body fat that causes so many health and self-esteem challenges.

There are those for whom diet works, though "dieting" never does, unless you hit upon a way of eating, which doesn't include starvation, that you are able and willing to continue for the rest of your life.

Dieting, in terms of simply cutting out part of your normal food intake, or eliminating certain foods for a while, rarely works long-term.

Note: This is partly because the section of your brain that decides to "go on a diet" is not the same part of your brain in charge of keeping the body in a steady supply of energy. That second part is on autopilot and will only put up with starvation so long before it turns into a beast that *will* get its way!

This is important for two reasons:

1. Cortisol is the stress hormone that causes your body to hold onto fat as a survival mechanism, so pitting one part of your body against another is self-defeating. Not only do you feel like crap emotionally, but it's also a surefire way to help keep that fat right where it is.

2. Don't blame yourself for your "lack of willpower," or other general weakness. It's part of why humankind has survived all these vast numbers of years, and it's way stronger than anyone's will, unless you are simply self-destructive.

Much better to work with your body than against it. Remember the catchphrase "Resistance causes pain." This is where it comes out in spades!

Others get results and swear by exercise as a way to release body fat, and again, that is individual. I took an aerobics class every Friday evening for 28 years (true story. Even included the same music from the '80s). Every Saturday morning my weight had dropped back to "'normal," i.e., minus the couple pounds that seemed to creep up during the week. I also remember how, when the class finally ended, my weight started to rise steadily. With this experience cemented into my "story," it's hard for me to accept there is not something to that…

One thing that seems consistent among proponents of both weight-training and more cardiovascular types of exercise is the idea of brief bursts of high-intensity exercise followed by short rest periods, repeated multiple times. In this way they claim 15-20 minutes of these alternating cycles jump-starts the metabolism to burn fat better than approximately an hour of more steady exercise.

There are hundreds of programs and experts who recommend cutting calories as the only way to lose weight, citing the fact that that muscle weighs more than fat, among other things. The more honest of them will recommend either very light exercise, or virtually none at all, stating "You won't have enough energy to work out under my calorie-reduction guidelines." OMG! Does anyone besides me find this crazy??

(Or else they keep mum about it and let you find out for yourself as you drag yourself through your food-deprived days—speaking from experience.)

The tapping (EFT) discussed in the Mind Clutter Chapter has proven extremely successful at helping people drop fat. On the surface level, it reduces stress, and its attendant stress hormone, cortisol (the fat-retaining hormone). Additionally, emotional blocks from "disliking" to "hating" ourselves for not being as slim as we'd like to be work in more subtle and convoluted ways to keep the weight on (What you resist persists—refusing to accept yourself as you currently are sets up internal battles you may not even be aware of, and which keep the weight on.) Whatever the reason, tapping helps remove the blocks, even in the absence of other dietary or exercise changes.

Colorado exercise trainer, Jill Johnson, noticed long ago that when her stress levels were high, her weight tended to rise as well. Through her research she came to believe it was the lack of oxygen in her body that led to the weight gain. This was because, as she puts it, "fat burns in the presence of oxygen," and when she was under a lot of strain she tended to breathe much more shallowly. I can vouch for that, having found my weight creeping up during periods of prolonged high-tension, high-deadline work, where I ended up hunched over my computer, barely breathing, for weeks on end.

She developed a style of exercise called "Oxycise," which combines a specific deep breathing technique along with tensing and holding different muscle groups for short periods. According to Johnson, the fat "burned off" with this technique stays off, not being subject to the variability of how people's metabolisms respond to dieting. Her training is unique, no-impact, and also helps build strength and flexibility.

Circling back to the "low-processed foods" discussion, word on the street is that the processed food industry deliberately puts addictive chemicals in their products so you don't want to stop at just one, and your stomach starts to look like a potato chip! Here's another good reason to declutter processed foods out of your life. If only they didn't taste so good! Waah!

To Supplement or Not to Supplement - Grumpy Is Optional

Ever find yourself going a little crazy trying to decide whether to take "vitamins," or any other of the bewildering variety of nutritional supplements available? If yes, which ones do you take? With oceans of advice freely dealt out about what's good for what physical condition, it's hard to know who to trust.

Declutter the idea that it's hopeless, so we might as well give up, or that there's no point making the effort.

The number of times over the years I've tried some new nutrient and found my body perking up on no uncertain terms has made it clear to me what a difference they can make. Other times I've tried something that was all the rage, only to have no reaction.

Nowhere is it more important to remember that each body is unique than with nutrition.

Some of the most successful drug and alcohol addiction treatments[19] include large amounts of specific vitamins, minerals, and amino acids. Successful meaning eliminating cravings and creating a much lower "return-to-substance" rate. It does this by repairing the ravages of extreme malnutrition brought on by consuming mass quantities of toxic substances, like, you know, alcohol and drugs for supper, instead of beer nuts and hot wings. OK, bad example. I really mean regular suppertime food.

I first heard about this when my life seemed, much to my surprise, to be chock full of alcohol addicts. I, myself, was not addicted to anything more grievous than movie nachos and could not bring myself to drink more than 1-2 drinks in an evening, no matter how hard I tried, but a startlingly large percentage of my homies were also alkies.

I learned that not only could these individuals be greatly "cured," or at least relieved of the most chemically dependent consequences of their addictions, but many other mental health challenges from both regular and postpartum depression to schizophrenia could be reduced, eliminated, or at least controlled using key supplements.

Talk about a rush! Imagine decluttering substance abuse or mental illness from your life with nutrition. Wow!

Naturally, I was curious about how well it worked. As I said, I couldn't test myself for curing a substance addiction. However, I had been noticing some depression in myself, unknown since pregnancy hormones. Some teeny, tiny thing would trigger me, and I would fall into the depths of despair, sobbing quietly, and feeling helplessly hopeless.

---

[19] I recommend *Seven Weeks to Sobriety* and *Depression Free Naturally* by Joan Larson, PhD.

I decided to try the recommendation for the most common type of depression (there are six, believe it or not), which included some vitamin C, and a handful of other common vitamins. The most intriguing was a B vitamin I hadn't heard of called "inositol." It came in a powder form that looks and tastes like powdered sugar. You were supposed to take ¼ teaspoon three times a day.

I tried the first dose in the evening, thinking to myself, "Well, this seems like kind of an *au natural* type treatment, so might take a couple weeks to notice."

It took twelve hours! One dose. Twelve hours. Depression gone. The pit of despair was filled in and leveled off. Something would happen that I expected to cause me to weep, and all I found was the empty set. Like a little kid trying to muster up some tears, I just couldn't seem to find any depression. It was almost comical.

I thought "Whoa! This is powerful!" Granted I was likely in better health than the average hardened drinker, having been into nutrition for about thirty years, but this was still staggering.

"How could this be?" I bet you're asking. Back to—"each body is unique." According to the advanced nutrition/mental health experts, some bodies need not just 100% of the minimum daily requirement of certain nutrients, but 1000%, or even more. If they get that unusual MDR met, they're OK. With some conditions, such as addictions, a few months of nutritional therapy returns the body chemistry back to factory settings, but with some of the more serious mental afflictions, it must be lifelong. It's a fascinating field, full of possibilities…

OK, so you're not struggling with paranoid schizophrenia, anorexia, or obsessive-compulsive disorder, only ordinary mood swings, PMS, or lack of energy. If these seem to have gotten worse over time, chances are your diet, no matter how organic, clean, and nutritious it might be, may need some supplementation to keep you in top form.

I eat fairly well, and as I said, I've sometimes been amazed at how much better I start feeling when I add in a new supplement.

For several years, I've been drinking a coffee infused with reishi mushroom extract, a food with some of the densest nutrition in the world (i.e., highest concentration of multiple nutrients per gram). According to pubmed.gov, a U.S. government website with links to vast numbers of medical and scientific studies worldwide (https://pubmed.ncbi.nlm.nih.gov/), reishi mushroom (*Ganoderma lucidum*) has been the subject of more than 2100 studies (at the time of this writing) which have explored its usefulness for multiple health conditions.

It gently detoxifies your bod, so it fits in neatly with clearing the space on your inside. Heck, all I care about is that my brain has gotten way sharper, my memory has returned to what it was in my 20s, my moods are smooth as cream, and I have a lot less wrinkles than I did ten years ago. Score!

Good way to declutter the vitamin stash:

You can really save yourself a ton of money and guesswork by consulting an expert who specializes in nutrition, and who uses testing techniques that pay attention to what YOUR body says it wants or needs.

This is one of those small sentences that has a huge impact. Not only can you save a lot of money, but knowing exactly what your body is short on, if anything, relieves an ocean of anxiety and guesswork, not to mention saving your liver the work of getting rid of what you don't need.

This could be a chiropractor who does muscle testing, a nutritionist who uses electronic testing (biomeridian[20]), blood

---

[20] Check out http://www.ahwcolorado.com/ for extremely thorough biomeridian testing.

testing, hair analysis, or other means. Orthomolecular physicians and other specialists also focus on nutrition and its effective use for resolving health issues.

Even a high-quality multivitamin recommended by a knowledgeable person at a health food store (not the least expensive one you can buy at a grocery store) can help you regain better energy, sleep, and calmness.

So, to answer the question, "To supplement or not supplement?", I say, yes, go right ahead if you are so inclined!

Exercise – What Your Body Loves

Exercise vs. Depression - Declutter the Blues

A few years ago, an article[21] appeared in the *New England Journal of Medicine* stating that exercise is, by a wide margin, the best way to treat depression. Not the millions of pills prescribed each year to combat it, nor the millions of hours of counseling (not to discount either of those, which have their value in certain situations), but plain old get-out-there-and-move-a-little.

Most of us have heard of the endorphins that kick in and make us feel so good, after about half an hour of exercise. Additional beneficial effects last for hours afterwards, even into the next day, with lowered heart rate and blood-pressure, and improved sleep, which also helps us feel better.

You can also mix up your workouts with activities that allow you to consciously breathe deeper, including walking; are all great for the lungs.

There's no law that says you must go to the gym to breathe deeper, you can do it cleaning the house, walking up and down

---

[21] Greer TL et al. Improvements in psychosocial functioning and health-related quality of life following exercise augmentation in patients with treatment response but nonremitted major depressive disorder: Results from the TREAD study. Depress Anxiety 2016 May 10

stairs at work or home, or sitting in front of the TV. For me, though, I never remember to do it as well as when an exercise instructor spurs me on.

It's easy to see that babies breathe deeply, and not hard to notice and be captivated by the way they do most everything with their whole bodies. It's because they are so tiny! Hard to move a muscle without moving the whole thing. You could take a page out of their book and look for exercises that involve your whole body. Luckily, there are many exercise options that do, yes?

My friend admitted he didn't really like any of the "workout at the gym" types of exercise, preferring hiking, dancing, and skiing. He probably would have been surprised to hear that I don't "like" them either, I just like how I feel after I'm done.

I do belong to a nice athletic club, and yes, before you jump to conclusions, I use it several times a week, and not just for the executive workout (shower and steam room).

My relationship with exercise has been a growing love over my lifetime, starting from near zero in my sedentary youth because all I ever really wanted to do was read. There were a few hikes in addition to my ill-fated backpacking trip, and hundreds of loathed gym classes at school.

Somewhere in my mid-teens, however, my younger sister and I egged each other on to work out to a booklet that appeared in our lives from who knew where—"The Canadian Air Force Exercise Program"—so I guess I wasn't completely hopeless/sedentary.

I grudgingly began to like getting in shape and expanded the consistency and extent of my exercise over many years, aided by learning more and more about the value of it. Though my club is not inexpensive, the cost is worth it, as without my sister there to help me I'm less likely to get the inspiration to work out on my own. And when I do, I don't push myself nearly as much as when I'm in a class.

I go to 4–5 classes a week, not just for the exercise, but to have company on the journey, hear interesting music, and see what new form of torture one of my instructors will come up with this time. Despite decades of classes, it never fails that each week somebody invents a new move. People are so creative! Since I much prefer variety to routine, this is what makes it bearable for me.

Several of my classes are yoga, which is huge on deep breathing. Taking even a few yoga classes will give you multiple benefits, not only for practicing breathing better, but for increased strength and flexibility.

Here's a little-known exercise secret which may help get you over that difficult hump of facing a workout. When I heard it, I thought, "What a relief to know." Here's the secret: If you feel like crap the first ten minutes of your workout, don't worry that you're a weak, pathetic, out-of-shape wimp. Absolutely everyone feels that way that way the first ten minutes—even the most seasoned, hard-core athletes. It's because it takes everyone's body that much time to start delivering the fuel (glycogen—you knew that) to the muscles.

Exercise doesn't have to be a barn-burner workout to be effective. Walking, again, is one of the best ways to exercise, and the fact that you've now heard this line approximately 1.3 million times doesn't make it any less true.

Another friend's extremely energetic 95-year-old mom and her twin sister are still going strong, though they've never seen the inside of a gym. Mom's house and gutters are spotless, as is her driveway when it snows. Unfortunately, one of her daughters (my friend's sister) recently passed away, in large part due to the very sedentary lifestyle she had led.

As always, it's what you like to do for exercise that's easiest to stick with, from yoga to walking to sports to hang-gliding. I like a variety, though I'll probably give hang-gliding a miss. I avoid boredom that way and give all my muscles a workout. But I am right up there in the ranks (me and the *NEJM*) of recommending exercise for depression. Whenever I start to feel a little down, I ask myself how long since I last worked out. It's usually been a minute and getting my mood back on track is just a half hour of exercise away.

Still, like my other friend who said, "Why run when you can walk? Why stand when you can lie down?", reflect on the practice of tai chi. Tai chi, a slow deliberate form of exercise, is the most active side of an overall practice called "qigong" (pronounced *chee-gong*). Along with passive seated activities including looking inward, relaxing the body, and breath work, tai chi is said to increase longevity (delay aging) by moving every muscle and joint in your body every day.

Below are two more exercise regimens that declutter the body. As it was explained to me, when our muscles become extremely tense from excessive strengthening exercises, the tendons that attach them to the bones, pull away slightly creating a void space where dead cells and other waste products accumulate. Since there is no method of circulation in these spaces pain can result. When you do either of these exercises (or get a massage) you are mechanically pressing that detritus out so the lymph fluid around the cells can pick it up and carry it away.

(By the way, you end up feeling extremely relaxed after these workouts, as with the massage, because the muscles are getting compressed, which triggers the brain to release relaxation chemicals. **This is the opposite and much more effective way to relax muscles than by stretching them, which triggers the brain to send out contraction remedies, and tenses you**

up more. Check out "pandiculation" for the full and mind-boggling story. Another vast myth busted!)

1. **Yamuna® Body Rolling** is a self-care and self-conditioning technique that uses specialized therapy balls to treat specific body parts. These soft, inflated balls range in size from softball to soccer ball size. By rolling on the balls, using your own body weight, you can address multiple layers of tissue, including skin, fascia, muscle, and bone, as well as work with connective tissues, internal organs, and the nervous system. It feels wonderful, like a massage, and you can take the balls with you anywhere.

2. **Feldenkrais – Declutter Your Joint Pain.** Developed by an Israeli engineer, these exercises for the spine and other joints are all about restoration; they are about relaxation and tension removal—the missing half (in American exercise culture) of strength and agility training. Each section of the spine in turn is allowed to relax off one side and then the other from a rolled-up firm blanket or mat placed under the spine. The exercises look simple, but are anything but, especially to someone who has tirelessly trained their muscles into the peak of athletic strength. The endless tension under which the muscles of a typical American athlete are held creates pressure and even deterioration in adjacent joints, tendons, and ligaments.

Your spine and other joints will gradually release the tension, even starting with the simplest basic version of this style of exercise. Eventually they feel amazing, as you continue with the practice, and they can improve spinal and other joint flexibility in nearly anyone of any age or condition.

If your work and lifestyle already include many hours on your feet and actively moving, the above two practices, as well as restore and yin yoga, will do a lot to ensure your body stays limber and strong at any age.

Simplify Your Medicine Cabinet

My medicine cabinet has long been decluttered to a box or two of adhesive bandages, a half empty bottle of cough syrup that I think expired ten years ago, and half an aspirin, also well past its sell-by date. I just don't seem to use anything from the thousands of items available over the counter.

For one thing, I take excellent care of myself, having incorporated much of what is covered in this chapter into my life routine. Everything isn't daily of course, aside from the eating, but I get around to most of it regularly, and it has paid off. I rarely become ill.

Recently I took a notion to double check the sun/shade growing requirement for a perennial I had bought to plant, called *Salvia pratensis*, which means meadow sage or meadow clary (gorgeous blue-purple spikes that get 3-5 feet tall(!), and so, so easy to grow, like most *Salvia*/sages. Yes, you should totally grow it!).

As we do, I wandered into the "used for" section and saw the essential oil of its cousin, clary sage, can be used for, among other things, red, inflamed eyes, and as a gargle for sore throats. Omigosh, where was I, after thrashing around the day before for far too long in a huge weed patch, and a chill breeze??

Red, inflamed eyes…check

Sore throat…check

And guess who happens to own a long-ignored bottle of therapeutic-grade clary sage essential oil? Me, of course. Good guess!

An hour later the sore throat was gone, using one drop of the essential oil. It took two applications to clear up the red eyes completely, and no, I didn't put them in my eyes, only below them.

Silly to be surprised, yet I still am continually awed by those magic substances, even fifteen years after I started using them. At the cellular level they work to raise the vibrational frequency of the body cells that have lowered, for whatever reason, into the "ill" range.

If you wanted to declutter your medicine cabinet, you could do a lot worse than acquire some therapeutic-grade essential oils and start learning what all they can be used for. They are the original multi-taskers, with each essential oil being helpful in assisting your body to heal from many different afflictions, such as the above-mentioned odd pair. This is because each essential oil contains multiple individual components, ranging from 70 to many hundreds, which work together synergistically. Most mainstream medicines start with essential oils, but the components are isolated and produced synthetically, which is why you get side effects. Without all the companion components, the body doesn't know what to do with these essentially foreign substances.

(By the way, and for example, clary sage essential oil has also traditionally been used for supporting hormone balance, fighting kidney disease, increasing circulation, insomnia, and relieving painful menstruation.)

Ever heard of gold, frankincense, and myrrh? The latter two are essential oils, and they, along with other essential oils, are mentioned about 500 times in the Bible (not one of my exaggerated statistics). Frankincense was used in Biblical times for everything from minor skin complaints to cancer, and many, many conditions in between.

Two Caveats

1. Note and warning: Essential oils are very powerful but can vary wildly in quality because of the way they are regulated in some of the countries they are produced. A bottle that says "100% essential oil," may only be 20% or even 5% essential oil, in reality. There are several reputable network-marketing companies and other online companies that sell therapeutic or premium-grade essential oils. They are usually pricier but far more effective.

   All others, including most sold in stores are diluted, sometimes to such a ridiculous extent, that there is almost no benefit left to them. (The effectiveness of all essential oils is immediately reduced by the addition of carrier oils, such as coconut, grapeseed, and jojoba. This can actually come in handy if you accidentally spill one on your skin that's a "hotter" one, such as oregano essential oil. Just grab the nearest vegetable oil, or skin lotion, to stop the burn.

2. A drop goes a long, long way, so use them in very small amounts, no more than a drop at a time, sometimes even less.

Declutter Your Stuff

If you want to know what's clutter's effect on your health: it hurts it.

The obvious basics include how much harder it is to clean around clutter, not to mention getting up the energy to clean in the first place, and the likelihood of clutter harboring dust bunnies and respiratory-system-challenging germs (or, you know, mice).

Multiple studies show clutter often invokes elevated levels of cortisol, the stress hormone. Nothing wrong with a little stress and cortisol from time to time, to keep you on your toes. (And regulate some important bodily functions.)

But clutter tends to be a constant irritant that exhausts the benefit of stress. Cortisol oversupply can lead to a host of symptoms—fatigue, digestive problems, difficulty in focusing, and many others, including (eek) weight gain in the belly area! (All right, that's it; clutter must go!)

Be Happy

What? Wait. Shouldn't this be in the "emotions" sections? I'm trotting out that circular nature of things agenda I bore down on much earlier.

Two Joseph things:

Joseph Pilates, German physical fitness trainer and developer of the "Pilates Method," was alive and teaching strong during the 1918–1920 Spanish flu pandemic that killed 50 million people worldwide. He noted that none of the people in his training classes contracted the flu. Modern research indicates exercise boosts immunity in multiple ways, from reducing inflammation, to increasing antibodies and reducing stress hormones (among many other benefits).

That last one caught my eye since it's the only one I can feel without going into the lab. Reduce stress hormones = raise endorphins! = feeling good! = feeling happy! = improved immune system!

Dr. Joe Dispenza's experiment described in Part I ("Back to the Rush") makes the connection between happier and healthier. Staggering to realize your own body has superior power to protect itself over human-made remedies, eh?

One more thing about habit and emotions. Much earlier we mentioned how we can get addicted to negative emotions as easily as vodka tonics, potato chips, or skydiving. It simply takes lots of practice, feeling angry or martyred, or whatever. It's a chemical brew. So, in order to get your body used to the chemical brew of happiness, and all the good things that can come out of that, both physically and in bettering your life through your own optimistic creativity, you need to practice that as well!

Practice looking for the good instead of the bad, practice smiling to yourself and others whenever you can, practice watching funny movies, practice taking yourself and others off the hook. **It doesn't come naturally. Fear comes naturally and through conditioning from life. It takes awareness and effort to get yourself into the happiness rut, but so worth the effort!**

Good Stress/Bad Stress

So, this is going to shock you. According to business researcher Shawn Achor, author of *Before Happiness* and *The Happiness Advantage*, stress and the hormones that go with it get such a bad rap; all we ever seem to hear about it is how bad it is for us and our health. **But, says Achor, there are an equal number of documented physical and psychological benefits to stress** that many of us aren't aware of.[22] What?!

---

[22] Achor, Shawn, *The Happiness Advantage: The Seven Principles of Positive Psychology that Fuel Success and Performance at Work*, "Skill 1: Reality Architecture: Choosing the Most Valuable Reality," Currency, 2014.

Stress has been shown to increase a sense of mastery (from overcoming an intense challenge), deepen relationships, strengthen priorities, increase appreciation for life, and increase a sense of meaning, among many other benefits. Focusing on an important deadline, for example, can actually increase the speed at which the brain processes information.

(You always suspected your best writing occurred as you put off your term paper till the last minute. Who knew you were right??)

His team worked with a large company that included 380 managers. Half the managers were shown a three-minute video on the many ways that stress is detrimental to human health. The other half were shown a similar video highlighting some of the ways that stress can be beneficial to us.

A week later several inventories were administered to the managers to assess productivity, quality of life, anxiety, etc. The "stress can be good" group experienced a 23% reduction in stress-related complaints, such as backache, headache, and fatigue, as compared to the "stress is bad" group, and their productivity increased by 30%! **These amazing changes were all simply the result of become aware of this new information about stress. No other changes at the workplace were implemented.**

This cracks me up, and makes me so happy…another myth up in flames!

The key to making stress work for you comes in recognizing the meaning behind the stress. You work hard at your job to provide for your family, for example. Also, remember "resistance causes pain," and when you stress about the stress, it can negatively impact your health.

Bonus Body Declutter Tip – Fire the Mirror Judge

Ever been blown away to hear family or friends tell you how beautiful/handsome/gorgeous you are? You think, "Are you talking to someone else? Are you on drugs? 'Cuz I looked in the mirror this morning, and what I saw was eyes a little too close together for comfort, one ear higher than the other, about six new wrinkles, blotchy skin, etc., etc."

OK, see, here's where that disconnect comes from. When we look in the mirror, we come to a screeching halt. We freeze-frame the face to maximize our ability to pull out the magnifying glass and examine every little "flaw" and "imperfection."

Thus, we manage to miss the most glorious part of our appearance, the part everyone sees but us—it's the vibrant energy, the nearly nonstop motion that everyone, even the calmest person, exudes.

It animates our features, speech, and moves, creating a magnetic quality that is almost irresistible to others. In short, it's our soul in action, and others can't help but say, "Hey, lookin' good!"

And, furthermore, ponder me this:

Thinking again about the cells of our bodies, the trillions of them, the thousands of chemical reactions that happen every second inside us, the miraculous transformation of two cells into a 200-pound human, for example, you could make quite a good case for spending your whole life in awe of your bod. Not starving it, browbeating it, resenting it, ignoring it, poisoning it, exhausting it, despising it, etc.

They say we're all just energy bundles anyway, so imagine how much energy could be freed up with all the effort we sink into putting our bodies down? What if, instead we simply said, "Holy crap, my body's freaking amazing!", and carried on with other matters? Well, it's a lot of energy freed up to play with!

PART V
THE BIG VIEW – FINAL THOUGHTS

Mind Clutter (Emotions and Thoughts), Revisited

To me, the biggest declutter of all when it comes to emotional baggage is the idea that we have no control over it. It turns out there are dozens of healthy strategies to work with our mental and emotional makeup to ensure it doesn't rule our lives.

Fear is behind most negative emotions. When outside life seems overwhelmingly scary, I try to **remember my heroes**, like the flight attendants (and, of course, the pilots) I referred to earlier. Here are a couple more:

Long, long ago, at a time when life seemed full of bombings and other terrifying events in the Middle East, I asked my friend who'd immigrated from there how in God's name everyday people coped with the strain? She said, "It's been going on so long, it seems normal. We just live with it. We plan our vacations, we celebrate our holidays, we live our lives." I adored her courage and have used it as an inspiration when life seems so hard, ever since.

My all-time favorite attitude hero:

A woman had been recently widowed from her beloved husband of many decades. Her children all lived far away from her, and they worried that she would be unbearably lonely. One

183

daughter urged her to move several hundred miles and be closer to her and at least a few other family members. The mother replied, "Even if I lost every single one of you, I would still make a life for myself, and it would be a good one!"

Woh! Smokin'!

Stuff Clutter, Revisited

Sooner or later, we get to the point of needing or wanting to declutter our unneeded, unloved possessions, with all their dragging down effects. Once we make our way through the sometimes-painful process of letting go of them, the exhilaration on the other side is wondrous to feel!

With all the decluttering tasks, it's still important to first declutter the guilts. Go easy on yourself! It does take awareness, practice, and patience. It's not instinctive. We're trained by life to be on the lookout for where we've gone "wrong," not what we've done "right."

Body Clutter, Revisited

The difference between ignoring your body's need for some decent nutrition and its need to move, versus decluttered eating and a decluttered body, is the difference between spending your golden years with one or more of the widespread degenerative diseases (almost all preventable) and a physically comfortable, active older age.

Since we can't stop a bad habit, but only replace it with a better one, give yourself credit for every step, no matter how tiny, in the direction you want to go.

And remember, your body is amazingly resilient! It gives you lots of chances. It's not always easy to get into the habit of eating your healthy veg, and getting some exercise, but it can be done with some practice and habit. Bribery?

And the Real You Shines Through – Once Again

Love this line: Today you have in front of you 100% of your life. Not the more familiar, "Today is the first day of the rest of your life!" (Sorry, that one sounds more like, "OK, be brave, it's not over yet, but you've already wasted a good part of it!" Maybe I'm looking on the dark side…).

Truth be told, if you are a new skater at age 45, and you dream of being an Olympic figure skating gold medalist, the odds are stacked against you. However, there's nothing that says you can't enjoy figure skating, and even competing, or having as much skating in your life as you want.

What if you're much older than 45? Still never too late to follow a dream. Louise Hay, founder of the enormously successful publishing company, Hay House, didn't start the company till she was in her sixties!

There are those who say the older you get the smarter you get, and the more life experiences you have, the better prepared you are to make a success of something that ambitious.

My body rolling instructor has had a student in her classes for over 20 years, whom she believes looks younger and livelier than when he started—in his sixties!

My Feldenkrais instructor told of an 80-year-old who first came into his class so hobbled with the effects of "old age" that he could barely get himself down to the mat on the floor, never mind getting back up. Four years and many classes later, he'd come in, throw the mat down, plop himself down, and make his way through the class and back to his feet with ease and grace.

Remember, too, with those dreams and desires you'd still like to tackle, it isn't only about the activities, it's about the unique way you approach them. There's no right way in that, whether laid-back or flat-out, it still comes down to who you are. Even if it's taken you 35 years to get on it—no guilt, 100% of your life is in front of you.

Decluttering and organizing allow the energized, real you to shine through! The best you can be, organized and clutter free! (If that's what works for you, that is.)

All those things make you who you are, which, in my opinion, is the meaning of life…to be who you are!

Counter-note:

After spending all these words encouraging you to shed your burdens of all kinds, it's good to remember, in the futility of resisting what is, that not all burdens are "bad." Releasing them, learning to deal with them, using them as a springboard to growth is part of being human. Of becoming who you really are.

Circling back to my backpacking experience, the real story is in all I learned from that tortuous week. The key phrase in all that was "half-heartedly training." I didn't really want to take that backpacking trip. My mom pushed me to do it, as she did every summer, to participate in the different camps available, rather than lie on my bed and read for three months—my preferred course of action.

My whiny attitude impacted how painful it was. The emotion was a much bigger burden than the 14 extra pounds of freeze-dried eggs and grape jelly I carried on this hardcore backpacking trip. In truth, only one of the dozen or so young teens on the trip was really in shape for it, so in typical teenage fashion we started complaining, and continued complaining all week long about anything and everything! It got so bad that by the fifth day one of the two adult leaders semi-yelled, "If you girls don't stop complaining, I'm going to walk out of here and leave you!"

So…like, we know she wouldn't really do that, but we also knew we darn well better stop complaining. And yowza! That's when I learned, once you get in a groove of complaining, even after only a few days, it is physically difficult to cease and desist!

You can bet I remembered the complaining lesson now cemented into my brain when I had my own teenagers. And, how lucky was I to learn it so early—a benefit of a stressful experience!

By the same token, I just had two further flashes of insight that never occurred to me in the intervening decades. One, my complaining, which wasn't actually typical for me, is fairly common among teenagers. So, I could choose to declutter the guilts about that. And two, I remembered my mom had absolutely loved the camps she went to as a teenager, so she was projecting her dreams onto mine, and assuming I'd have as much fun. Not my style, hers.

However, honesty compels me to admit I'm glad I had the miserable experience for so many reasons, not the least of which is learning, in a physical way, the joy of decluttering your pack and lightening your load. I also need to admit that though I resisted the "camps" idea every time, those experiences are some of the best remembered of my childhood. Without knowing it (or maybe she did), Mom was helping me get out of my shell, and take on more of life's adventures!

The Biggest Aha! – Secret Bonus Tip

Remember back in Part I when I mentioned Dr. Joe Dispenza's experiment about how the strength of the participants' immune systems increased substantially from just four days of practicing happy emotions for thirty minutes a day?

Around the same time I was reading this, I took an outdoor yoga class on the lawn at my athletic club. At the end of the class, we were lying on our backs in the relaxation pose that is the final pose in nearly every yoga class (shavasana). The idea is to relax every single muscle in your body in order to absorb the benefits of the practice.

That sounds like a job to me, so instead I just revel in the relaxation, full stop. It feels so, so delicious after a yoga workout, which can be a lot more strenuous than you might think. The instructor had a sweet, *super* soothing voice, and she was playing ever-so-gentle yoga music. Then, to top it off we were peering up through the branches of a summer tree, watching the sunlight dance through the bright green lacy leaves!

Talk about endorphins! Talk about a rush! Talk about the perfect setting and multiple scrumptious sensory inputs to bring that yummy feeling on!

Then, all of a sudden, I got a jolt of realization that stopped me cold.

I knew in that moment that even with all that perfect setup for bliss, and all those delicious sensations coming from the outside world, the main ingredient in my blissful feeling was my own endorphins swimming around inside me.

I was the one who released the endorphins! Not the shavasana, not the instructor, not the music, not the sun-dappled leaves! Me! I created the rush!

From there it was a short step to the further realization that I could also choose to remember that moment anytime, anywhere, and feel the same bliss!

If you missed that yoga class I went to, or any yoga class for that matter, you can simply remember something that makes you feel good; something funny, or something adorable in one of the children/pets in your life, or how it feels when someone first puts their hands on you for a backrub, or you've just finished those 30 minutes of exercise and are happily heading for the shower, or you've just taken your first bite of lemon meringue pie, or cleaned out your closet, or any of the hundreds of other stimuli that give you a feeling of bliss.

Beyond the Rush

After that experience, I took one more step in my thought process and it dawned on me: I didn't even need to remember that scrumptious scene. I could release the endorphins myself, anytime, anywhere! It's totally in my control![23]

I don't have to wait till I've meditated, or completely decluttered my house, or prioritized my to-do list, or achieved all my goals, or walked half an hour every day, or released all my guilt, or eaten X grams of fiber per day.

I also don't have to have a big glass of wine, buy new shoes, gossip about my boss, wallow in front of the TV, or run away to Tahiti.

I don't have to do any of these things, either "good" or "bad," to create the rush. All I have to do is practice being happy, letting the endorphins (the rush) swirl through my body. It's under my control to feel at peace, to supercharge my immune system, and to improve my health!

Clear the Space, Revisited

One of my clients said, "On Saturdays I long to do some fun activity like hiking, or checking out a museum I haven't seen, as a break from my work week. But then I always think, 'First, I should do something with that stuff in the guest room.' I call it 'guest room,' but no one could stay there since it's full of boxes

---

[23] Note: If you decide to delve into Dr. Dispenza's book (*Becoming Supernatural*, etc., there's a meditation called "Blessing of the Energy Centers Meditation" on page 111 which put me way ahead in experiencing how I could switch on my own endorphins. It feels delicious, too!

I still haven't unpacked from our last move. But I dread it so much I never really get in there to start, so what actually happens is, I don't end up doing either one."

I asked her how long since they'd moved. She replied, "Ten years." (!?!)

A medical IT person with grown children, she lives with her husband and a couple head of cats in a lovely suburban home with mostly tidy spaces, but that one room drags her down like the proverbial ball and chain. Kind and conscientious, she is already thinking ahead to what her children will have to deal with, stuff-wise, when she and the mister go to heaven.

Not only that, but her emotions are also cluttered up by feelings of being nearly a prisoner to these mighty objects, and her body is missing out on the exercise and action that a free Saturday might bring. The same exercise and action could also inspire her to come home and pitch out all that ten-dollar junk lurking in the guest room. As usual, one dovetails with the other.

Decluttering and organizing clear the space in your home, your heart, and your body for those frisky adventures or giant aspirations you long to tackle, and free up the energy to achieve them. It's about making the best of your life; expressing the best of who you really are—your talents and passions, and about living life to the fullest!

Clearing the space is awesome and so worth the effort. It gives you back the power to make your life as great as it can be, both for yourself and for all those around you, who are lucky enough to have you in their lives!

ACKNOWLEDGMENTS

To Brian Schwartz, kind and experienced publisher, thanks for insisting, with heart, I do my best work, along with diligent editor, Daniel Siuba, and the rest of the Wise Media Group team. Tatiana Fernandez, thanks for rockin' cover design; you nailed it!

Thanks, Tamley Eierdam, Judi Filler, and the rest of your panel for helping me revamp the beginning to much greater effect. Thanks, Anita Edge, for the same, and for always keeping me in the loop internet marketing-wise. To Sheri Anspach, computer expert and Reiki master, thanks for keeping me going as I wore out laptop after laptop.

Angela Schnaubelt, your suggestions on what to put first made all the difference!

Thanks to Jon Haass for loaning me a huge, temporarily empty office and 20 empty desks to spread out my pages and see the whole picture. It was a turning point, *and* a chance to be a tycoon for a few days. I liked it!

To Michelle Dashnaw, Leigh Lasik, and Janice Mueller (best of sisters!) thanks for providing inciteful comments, and for believing in me. (And to Charlie Mueller, best of brothers-in-law, thanks for being you! And for modeling how uncluttered spending can lead to excellent outcomes, i.e., early retirement.)

Thanks to Dr. Larry Quell, and to the Yuen group (Jerry, Kathy, Karole, Adrienne, Pegi, Pamela, and Lydia) for helping me keep my energy decluttered through the years. Thanks to Tony, for cheering me down the home stretch, and politely reminding me I was repeating myself, whining-wise.

To Rod Smith, Barry Overton, Jonathan Manske, Chuck Blakeman, and Angel Tuccy, thanks for the hours and hours of training, inspiration, and entertainment you tirelessly provided. You got your books done before me, so I had to catch up. To Maurice Washington, my birthday brother, thanks for giving me the idea for "feel the rush," whether you realized it at the time or not.

To Rollande Lockhart, best of stepmoms, thanks for your much-appreciated unique twist on things. You always know what to say! Thanks to you, as well as Esther and Jerry Ellefson, for showing the value of resilience and optimism in the face of adversity.

Thanks Nancy Griffin, for "volunteering" me to give that talk. It led to my biggest a-ha moment. You'll never know what that did for me. Thanks to two of my oldest friends, Elaine Walford and Robbie Zephirin, for showing me blondes can have more fun, *and* still be brainy, and organized! To Marilou Kiessig, Head Cheerleader, you have the world's biggest heart! Thanks for supporting me, and also modeling "assumed success."

To my amazing sons, Ben and Ian, you turned out just as I hoped – kind, energetic, resourceful, courageous, and humorous. Thanks for being willing to lend a hand when I needed it, for encouraging me not to give up this project, and for cracking me up! To my daughters-in-law, Jamie and Jenn, thanks for shining in your own lights, for modeling strength and kindness to my sweetest of grandgirls, and for taking good care of my boys.

Thanks to Mom and Dad, for always telling me I could do whatever I put my mind to (and for not getting after me for how long it took.) Though no longer with me in person, your encouraging words remain.

To family, friends, and clients, thanks for the stories, insights, and examples you gave me. I love to learn from you and admire your courage in learning to let go, and also to acknowledge what really matters for you to keep.

If I left anyone out in my acknowledgments, please know you are still deeply appreciated!

ADDITIONAL RESOURCES

Mind Clutter

Achor, Shawn, *Before Happiness: The 5 Hidden Keys to Achieving Success, Spreading Happiness, and Sustaining Positive Change,* Currency, 2013.

Achor, Shawn, *The Happiness Advantage: The Seven Principles of Positive Psychology that Fuel Success and Performance at Work,* Currency, 2014.

Allen, David, *Getting Things Done, The Art of Stress-Free Productivity,* Penguin Books, 2001.

Aslett, Don, *Done! How to Accomplish Twice as Much in Half the Time – at Home and at the Office,* Adams Media, 2005.

Barrett, Lisa Feldman, *How Emotions Are Made; the Secret Life of the Brain,* Mariner Books, 2017.

Blakeman, Chuck, *Re-Humanizing the Workplace (By Giving Everybody Their Brain Back),* Crankset Publishing, LLC 2021.

Chamine, Shirzad, *Positive Intelligence, Why Only 20% of Teams and Individuals Achieve Their True Potential, and how you can Achieve Yours,* Greenleaf Book Group Press, 2016.

Dispenza, Dr. Joe, *Becoming Supernatural, How Common People Are Doing the Uncommon,* Hay House, 2017.

Manske, Jonathan, *The Law of Attraction Made Simple: Magnetize your Heartfelt Desires,* Books To Believe In, 2008.

Miedaner, Talane, *Coach Yourself to Success, 101 Tips from a Personal Coach for Reaching Your Goals at Work and in Life,* Contemporary Books, 2000.

Neill, Michael, *Supercoach, 10 Secrets to Transform Anyone's Life,* Hay House Inc., 2010 and 2018 Editions.

O'Hanlon, Bill, *Do One Thing Different, and Other Uncommonly Sensible Solutions to Life's Persistent Problems,* William Morrow and Company, Inc., 1999.

Overton, Barry, *Ignite Your Greatness, The Secret to Lighting the Fire Within,* Barry Overton/Overton Unlimited, 2020.

Pritchett, Price, PhD, *The Quantum Leap Strategy,* Pritchett, LP, 2006.

Pritchett, Price, PhD, *You², A High-Velocity Formula for Multiplying Your Personal Effectiveness in Quantum Leaps,* Pritchett, LP, 2012.

Ruiz, Don Miguel, *The Four Agreements, A Practical Guide to Personal Freedom, A Toltec Wisdom Book,* Amber-Allen Publishing, Incorporated, 1997.

Slatter, Jean, *Hiring the Heavens, A Practical Guide to Developing Working Relations with the Spirits of Creation,* New World Library, 2003.

Smith, Rod, *The Rod Effect, Dreaming 2.0, Master 8 Philosophies That Took Me from the Projects to NFL Super Bowl Stardom,* Black Card Books, 2017.

Susanka, Sarah, *The Not So Big Life, Making Room for What Really Matters,* Random House, 2007.

Tuccy, Angel, *Lists that Saved my Life,* Create Space, 2009.

Possessional Clutter

Culbertson, Judy and Decker, Marj, *Scaling Down, Living Large in a Smaller Space,* Rodale Press, 2005.

Culp, Stephanie, *Organized When You Don't Have the Time, A Simple 5-Step Approach That Will Fit Even the Busiest Schedule,* Writer's Digest Books, 1986.

Culp, Stephanie, *Streamlining Your Life: A 5-Point Plan for Uncomplicated Living,* F&W Media, 1995.

Jones, Peggy and Young, Pam, *Sidetracked Home Executives, From Pigpen to Paradise,* Balance, 2001.

Kingston, Karen, *Clear Your Clutter with Feng Shui, Free Yourself from Physical, Mental, Emotional, and Spiritual Clutter Forever,* Random House, Inc., 1999.

Kondo, Marie, *The Life-Changing Magic of Tidying Up, The Japanese Art of Decluttering and Organizing,* Ten Speed Press, 2014.

Morgenstern, Julie, *Organizing from the Inside Out, The Foolproof System for Organizing Your Home, Your Office, and Your Life,* Henry Holt and Company, LLC, 1998.

Smallin, Donna, *Organizing Plain and Simple, A Ready Reference Guide with Hundreds of Solutions to Your Everyday Clutter Challenges,* Storey Publishing, 2002.

Stack, Laura, *Leave the Office Earlier, The Productivity Pro Show You How to Do More in Less time…and Feel Great About It,* Broadway Books, 2004.

St. James, Elaine, *Simplify Your Life,* MJF Books, 2001.

Walsh, Peter, *It's All Too Much, An Easy Plan for Living a Richer Life With Less Stuff,* Free Press, 2007.

Winston, Stephanie, *Stephanie Winston's Best Organizing Tips, Quick Simple Ways to Get Organized – and Get on With Your Life,* Simon & Schuster, 1995.

Physical Body Clutter

Caras, Dr. Nick, and Tuccy, Angel, *Sex, Drugs, & Rock N Roll, 3 Keys for a Healthier Lifestyle,* Create Space, 2010.

Douillard, John, *The 3-Season Diet, Eat the Way Nature Intended: Lose Weight, Beat Food Cravings, Get Fit,* Three Rivers Press, 2000.

Johnson, Jill, *Oxycise, How anyone can get rid of fat forever in only 15 minutes a day with the power of oxygen!* Oxycise International, 1997.

Larson, Joan Mathews, PhD., *Seven Weeks to Sobriety, The Proven Program to Fight Alcoholism Through Nutrition,* Random House Publishing Group, 1992.

Larson, Joan Mathews, PhD., *Depression-Free, Naturally: 7 Weeks to Eliminating Anxiety, Despair, Fatigue, and Anger from Your Life,* Random House Publishing Group, 1999.

Ortner, Jessica, *The Tapping Solution for Weight Loss and Body Confidence, A Woman's guide to Stressing Less, Weighing Less, and Loving More,* Hay House, Inc., 2014.

Ortner, Nick, *The Tapping Solution: A Revolutionary System for Stress-Free Living,* Hay House, 2013.

Strand, Ray D, M.D., *Healthy for Life, Developing Healthy Lifestyles that Have a Side Effect of Permanent Fat Loss,* Real Life Press, 2005.

Schwarzbein, Diana, M.D., *The Schwarzbein Principle, The Truth About Losing Weight, Being Healthy and Feeling Younger,* Health Communications, Inc., 1999.

13930759R00125